CL. Reddon

CONTENTS

A DEFINITIVE GUIDE TO BUILDING A SUCCESSFUL MARRIAGE

DIG DEEP
BEFORE
YOU LEAP

EXPANDED EDITION

CRITICAL FACTORS TO EXPLORE
BEFORE ENGAGING IN MARRIAGE

CL. REDDON

Library of Congress Control Number: 2023906577

ISBN: 979-8-9867162-3-7 (paperback)
ISBN: 979-8-9867162-4-4 (hardcover)
ISBN: 979-8-9867162-5-1 (eBook)

Studio, Canva Creative, Simple Pink and Plum Background Love Quote, Canva.com.

Zaebab, Blue Dark Minimalist Initial E Logo, Canva.com.

Cover Design by HubSpot Pro
Text Design by C8V_Logos (Fiverr)
Photography by Roy Cox

First printing edition 05/08/2023

Electric Capricorn Media
23415 Three Notch Rd, Suite 2008 #122,
California, Maryland 20619

www.clreddon.com

DIG DEEP

BEFORE

YOU LEAP

**ELECTRIC
CAPRICORN**
Publishing

——DEDICATION——

To my beloved Karen...

Thank you for always supporting and encouraging me to pursue my passions and dreams. Your unwavering love and guidance have been the foundation of my success and accomplishments. This book is dedicated to you, with the deepest gratitude and admiration for your unwavering commitment to my growth and well-being. Your love and support have been a constant source of inspiration, and I am forever grateful for all that you have done for me.

With all my love and appreciation,

C.L. Reddon

INTRODUCTION

I n a society filled with broken marriages, families, and dreams, the last thing we need is another example of a married couple that could not get the institution of marriage right. Unfortunately, we are provided with poor examples daily. We can often find more examples of relationships gone wrong than unions on the right path in our homes, schools, churches, and even on our television screens. In that regard, no relationship is without flaws. As a matter of fact, no relationship will ever be flawless. That does not, however, mean we should stop striving for perfection.

A failed marriage, in my opinion, is more likely to be caused by issues that existed at the beginning of a romance than by issues that developed later on. In the fall of 2007, with my marriage over, I found myself sitting on my parents' floor, crying my eyes out for the same reasons I just described.

I too, like so many, married for the wrong reasons. I married simply because I thought once I did, all of the issues that I had been hiding from as an adult would disappear. I figured that if I focused my energy and attention on a new wife, making her happy, and helping her through her circumstances, I would eventually resolve my own. In the end, my calculations proved to be inaccurate. Added to the regret of this episode in my life is that I miserably failed at choosing the right partner ten years before my second attempt into marriage. Yes, that's correct! The wrong reasons led me to get married on not one but two separate occasions.

After my second divorce, I thought long and hard about the relationship failures in my life, as well as similar failures experienced by others. Undoubtedly, the individuals who have experienced divorce cannot all be bad people, can they? The answer to that question is no. Unfortunately, as with so many other things in life, we lack the necessary training, guidance, tools, and information before undertaking any new endeavor. As a result, people want what they want. As such, they do not often read the fine print. This is true of people purchasing cell phones, cars, and houses. Typically, for the things in life that we believe are needs, we sign our names on the dotted lines because the need at the time trumps the underlining things we need to know.

Sadly, this is why we take losses in so many areas of our lives. We do not take the time to read the fine print or consult someone who can explain the finer details to our cluttered minds. In the same way that people agree to service contracts without reading them carefully and paying attention to the details, it's common for people to enter into relationships without paying attention to the particulars. We see it, like it, and sign up for it. We do not ask any questions. We do not pose ourselves any questions. We do not consider the risk. And in most respects, it does not seem like we care about them. This is why pharmaceutical companies are raking in huge profits on drugs that suppress HIV/AIDS. It is because people are engaging in behaviors without considering the risk. This is why divorce lawyers will never be out of work. Many individuals are willing to roll the dice on anything they desire in life before examining the pros and cons of the outcome. When it comes to marriage and divorce, the names and stories change, and the circumstances, to some degree, are different. Still, my friend's characteristics are precisely the same underlying themes for what sinks relationships.

Regardless of a person's status, place in life, education, color, creed, or any other attribute you might be able to summon to your mind, the experience of divorce is enough to make any person crumble to their knees. I have seen the strongest men and fiercest women weep like babies at the end of a marriage. Why do people cry, you ask? Well, people become emotional for a variety of reasons. As for me, it was the sheer embarrassment of having to inform family and friends just a few months after our wedding that my bride and I were no longer together. Additionally, it was the fact that I did not have the financial means to rent an apartment. This is a time in my life when it would appear that most of my active funds were allocated to inactive relationships. Clearly, a series of poor decisions contributed to this outcome. Besides these details, I realized that I had lived nearly half my life expectancy, I had nothing to show for it, and had to either move back home with my parents or accept homelessness.

In my view, this period of my life was the start of my turning point. It was indeed a humbling experience. But it was a period of my life that taught me a harsh lesson. In any aspect of life that you can imagine, when you call yourself taking the easy route or the path of least resistance, you are only making a more challenging road for yourself at some point in your future. My ignorance regarding pertinent matters related to money, credit, parenting, being a provider, an effective communicator, and a well-rounded person, all of these flaws revealed themselves in both my failed marriages. The attributes that I just listed were not only true for me. But they were also confirmed in one way or the other with the women I married.

They did not know enough about me, and I certainly did not know enough about them. My two former wives and I shared a similar ignorance regarding life, love, and relationships, which inspired me to write this book. I reversed engineered my mistakes and examined countless other cases involving couples, marriage, and divorce, and arrived at some conclusions that I found beneficial for our collective understanding of relationships and marriage. Toxic relationships and marriages like those experienced in my lifetime do not have to be. In order to prevent this from occurring, some elements concerning life need to be acquired, while other traits must be jettisoned. To create the type of marriage God wants you to have for the purpose, He has intended, you will need to end many of the socially accepted behaviors that are commonplace today. Creating the type of marriage acceptable in God's sight means that you must immediately refrain from behaviors undoubtedly posed to ruin your relationship while causing yourself significant discomfort.

When most people decide to get married, they often base their decision to wed on what they feel and not necessarily what they can prove. With that said, any relationship built on fraudulent information or details is a relationship that will not last. The ignorance we have regarding the people we marry, eventually sleep with, and conceive children is dangerous. If we are not willing to investigate the person's background for whom we are promising to marry, how do we know that someday that person will not be the one to end our existence on earth?

Now, as farfetched as this might sound, this is a more sad reality for people than you might think. If you do not believe this is true, feel free to search your favorite search engine, type in the phrase 'women killed by boyfriend,' and then settle yourself in for some heartbreaking stories and gruesome statistics. People are tying the knot without knowing much about their tolerances, likes or dislikes, and even less about the person they are determined to be with for the rest of their lives. One of the number one causes of divorce involves infidelity or what many might call a lack of commitment. If you are not asking pointed questions to determine a potential spouses' tolerance, how do you know that person will be committed in a relationship? How do you know that they will be faithful in marriage?

If infidelity is the number one cause for divorce, issues involving money matters must be listed as 1A. How many folks do you presume to get married without knowing anything about their partner's credit, spending habits, or how they earn their money? How many people engage in romantic relationships with those who lack a job or good credit but do so because of contributing factors associated with low self-esteem? Thus, ignoring one of the most impactful factors in any relationship? Accordingly, based on the reasons outlined in this prologue, this text was written. In truth, many people like myself have married and divorced multiple times without consideration of any of the information you are about to read.

I hate to admit it, but much of what we have been taught about relationships and, to a large extent, life, in general, is fiction, fairytales, and mythology. If I may be very candid, no one is going to save you from yourself, your lack of knowledge, or your self-inflicted circumstances. This is a job that is exclusively yours. To attract the perfect mate, you must become their perfect match. Being the perfect spouse requires preparation.

And to be clear, none of this is about your appearance, how well you smell, how well you cook, or how many sexual positions you can perform from the ceiling fan. What I am describing has to do with an individual's character.

Your personal development means that you have worked on the things that make you an asset as a partner and not a liability. You see, that is what I was in both my failed marriages. I was a huge liability. At the time, I really thought that my efforts made me an asset in their lives. I was mistaken. I was not an asset at all. I was just a fool. And for some people entering relationships, their entrance into a presumed love affair is all about the chores that they are looking to have some fool to do. This book was written to ensure that you do not end up in a relationship where you are not loved, respected, or valued.

This happens to be where I found myself so many years ago. Through counseling, I learned that the biggest failure in my relationships was myself. Additionally, I had to accept that my role in not picking the right people to love was on me. I expected people to give me something that I did not pick them to do. If you want freshly squeezed orange juice for breakfast, why would you go out to purchase a barrel of tomatoes? If we choose people for purposes other than love, respect, and honor, we can expect those same people to give us things that do not include the aforementioned characteristics.

In this regard, this is why I believe the expression that a good man or woman is hard to find is nonsense. How can a person rightfully define a good man or woman if they are not one themselves? How can a person declare what a good man or woman is when they have only been looking for sexual partners or glorified roommates? In my opinion, most people would not be able to tell the difference between a good man and a good woman even if someone stood directly in front of them with a sign around their neck declaring such. As a matter of fact, I believe that this is true because the characteristics of what it means to be a decent, kind, compassionate, caring, and unselfish individual are not taught, explained, exhibited, or revealed to us during our formative years. If we are honest, it is not reflected in the more significant portion of society from which we originate.

The expression "good man" or "good woman" is often used as a turn of phrase in our society. But the definition of what makes a man or woman good, well, that definition is hidden in plain view. For this reason, many people are blind. I hope that my story and a few antidotes shared in the book will raise your awareness to what you may have been missing in your current relationship and bring your attention to what you should be aspiring to have moving forward. Based on the advice of a late pastor, the title of this book is derived from his regular advice to his congregation to consider their actions before taking them.

Dig Deep Before You Leap Defined

As implied by its name, "Dig Deep Before You Leap" is simply a reminder to "Think Before You Act." This principle can be applied to many aspects of life. Additionally, the title highlights the importance of looking beyond the surface of what is visible to discover truths that can only be found through wisdom and a sincere desire for righteousness. The book emphasizes the necessity of looking beyond the appearances of others. It also highlights the need to focus on the inner characteristics that may contribute to success or failure.

Looking Beyond The Appearances

This in itself is going to be difficult. Essentially, you will need to retrain your mind to do something different than what it has been shown to do. In our modern society, the emphasis is always put on how a person looks. When most individuals start the process of looking for a companion, there is no fundamental importance placed on the character of the individual. Typically, the first things considered have to do with physical characteristics.

This is the blueprint that most of us have followed. For that reason, it is a learned behavior that we must put on the back burner in this effort. This book will teach you how to look beyond an individual's appearance, and using pointed questions, guide you towards the underlying truths buried beneath the soil, facts that will reveal the unseen or hidden characteristics of who and what your potential spouse might be.

Focus On The Inner Characteristics

Once the hidden characteristics are known, you will be allowed to make relationship decisions based on facts rather than the fictionalized conclusions often created on visual appearances and topical suppositions alone. You will accomplish this effort using a three-pronged strategy that I have found invaluable. The approach I am referring to involves research, investigation, and evaluation. During the research phase, you will gather the details needed to assess your relationship with an individual. Once you have gathered the information, you will then investigate your findings. After studying the facts you have found complete, you will evaluate the results and render your decision.

It must be understood that the first person required to go through this process will be yourself. You can't possibly know what is right for you or who is suitable for you unless you know yourself. Now, this piece of information is priceless. Fact! Most people enter relationships with no clue, direction, and purpose. Essentially, they get involved in a relationship hoping that their partner can not only guide them through the relationship process but that they can also help them find themselves. Can you imagine a person going into your local convenience store and the clerk saying, "Can I help you find something?" And the person saying, "I don't know what I am looking for?" This is what often happens in relationships.

We show up in them, get inside their doors, and have no clue why we are there, what we are looking for, what we need, require, or demand. We are just there. And staying with the convenience store analogy, if the clerk feels that we are wasting their time, we are asked to leave. Why is this the case? It is because we are not allowing someone who has a clear understanding of what they need, want, require, and demand to occupy that valued real estate. In the same way, convenience stores are in business to be successful; we should be looking for partners that give us success in the relationship space.

In life, many of us miss the mark because we are not positioned for the things we want, need, require, or demand.

Unfortunately, most people live their entire lives out of position. We are locked into jobs outside of our natural positions, involved in groups, clubs, or organizations, and are interested in relationships outside our position.

This book teaches you how to get into a position for a successful relationship. To get into your proper position, you must first know your purpose for wanting to be in a relationship in the first place. Why do you want to be in a relationship? Why do you want to get married? Why do you want to marry your potential spouse? What about them makes you feel safe, secured, and protected? How do you know if these feelings are genuine? And speaking of your potential spouse, why should they want to marry you?

Have you asked? These are purpose questions. If you don't know your purpose for anything, you are already out of position.

Additionally, what type of value will you bring to your relationship? What intangibles do you offer that cannot be purchased from your local big-box store or online? This is another area that most people in relationships never stop to consider. Am I bringing value to the relationship? Am I getting value from the relationship? Am I getting value from my partner in this relationship? These are three questions that most people never consider.

To be successful in this enterprise, you need to think of yourself as a relationship detective. Your primary responsibility in this season of your life is to investigate matters related to your heart and the hearts of those suitors interested in occupying your relationship space. In this role, you must operate using the disciplines below.

You must be an:

- Examiner
- Reviewer
- Auditor
- Researcher
- Scrutinizer
- Appraiser
- Inspector
- Checker
- Adjudicator
- Monitor
- Tester
- Arbiter
- Analyzer
- Questioner
- Observer
- Explorer
- Interviewer
- Verifier

Now I know this might seem like a daunting task. Some people may believe that getting involved in a relationship shouldn't require this type of detail or effort. As I said earlier, relationships are real. They are not the makings of fairy tales and mythology. I believe these measures are essential because of the fundamental nature of relationships and what is often at stake when we fail to do our due diligence in protecting ourselves from hurt, harm, or worse.

To be clear, this is a premarital investigation guide. It outlines the need for premarital investigation in various forms, emphasizing the importance of premarital counseling. In my view, if you miss any of these steps, you are creating a potential burden for your life that is not only unnecessary, but it is unavoidable.

Lastly, this book is not intended to be a replacement for marriage counseling, therapy, or anything of the sort. This work is simply a supplement to those other sources. With that said, I strongly encourage you to seek out advice from a licensed therapist, clergy member, or counselor at your house of worship. In the end, I hope my story and what I have learned in my journey helps you to avoid many of the pitfalls that I have experienced. I wish you and your potential spouse much success in your relationship endeavors.

"Love suffers long and is kind; love does not envy; love does not promote itself, is not puffed up, does not behave badly, seeks not her own, is not easily "but rejoices in the truth; bears all things, believes all things, hopes all things, endures all things. Love never fails."

1 Corinthians 13:4-8

Chapter

1

THE STAR
OF A STORY

When I first conceived the idea to author a book about marriage and the need for couples to consider premarital investigation before getting married, I thought to myself, I have lost my mind. Why would anyone take advice from someone who has been divorced twice? Ultimately, I accepted that I was not just equipped to serve as a warning to those considering marriage, but that I had a responsibility to do so. In life, we benefit significantly from the experiences of others, both positive and negative. As an example, none of us were alive when Thomas Edison invented the light bulb.

Nevertheless, we all benefit greatly from his invention. In this way, the experiences of others can be used to remedy the social ills of humanity as a whole. As Edison invented the bulb to illuminate the darkened corridors of the world, God has given me the divine insight necessary to write this practical guide. Having gained wisdom from my experiences with relationships, including marriage and divorce, I believe people can benefit greatly from my perspective and my story. Therefore, I am ideally suited to discuss the dire need for premarital investigation and counseling, and I wish to share this information with you.

Perhaps you are wondering how I became an expert on the subject of premarital investigation, counseling, and its importance. That can be answered in one word: DIVORCE! The catalyst for my expertise in premarital investigations, counseling, and their necessity is attributed to my experiences with divorce. In my view, if anyone tells you that divorce is not difficult, then you are probably talking to someone who does not know what they are talking about. Having a divorce is as agonizing as undergoing surgery of any sort without the use of anesthesia.

Some people think marriage and divorce are as straightforward as one, two, three. This is not the case. When it comes to divorce, it does not matter if a couple was married seventy-two years or seventy-two days, saying good-bye, and ending a relationship is never easy. It was not easy for me the first time I made my way through the process, and it certainly was not any easier the second. There is no doubt that my story with regard to divorce is that of a two-time loser. So, before we delve into the specifics of premarital investigation, let me briefly give you a bit of background on who I am and how I became an unlucky authority on this subject.

Turn Around

In my early childhood, Teddy Pendergrass' smash hit "Love TKO" dominated the airwaves. It remains one of his most popular songs.As told in this timeless classic, the late crooner tells the tale of a man who has many problems with relationships, love, and lust. As with every generation, today's music consumers seldom, if ever, pay close attention to the lyrics of a song, instead focusing on its hook and melody. When I was a child, this was certainly the case. Imagine my surprise when I heard this tune 20 years later on the radio while driving to court to finalize my divorce. The pain, hurt, and emotional turmoil of this man's life became my own.

It is often said that women make up their minds to leave a man months before they say the words. If this is true, my second marriage was over the day she signed the marriage license. You may be asking yourself, "How is it that someone who has experienced divorce once can repeat the same mistake twice?" Well, the answer is simple. Stupidity! There was one common denominator in both of my failed relationships: me. I was not forced into marriage by either woman. My decision was not influenced by any pending pregnancies or threats.

Neither of my marriages were compelled by acts of violence. During both instances, I made unwise choices based on the following reasons:

- Feelings of Rejection
- Feelings of Loneliness
- Desire for Sex
- Low Self-Esteem
- Narcissistic Personality Disorder (NPD)
- Personal Failures

Find It In Your Heart

Usually, adults struggling with issues such as these can trace their anxiety back to their adolescent years. In my case, I can remember being huskier than the other children. In grade school, I was often teased about my size. Throughout my primary and intermediate school years and well into high school, I was pretty insecure, especially regarding the opposite sex. However, it was a whole new ball game after I graduated high school and entered college. Like most college students, I worked various gigs to pay the bills.

When I was a young teenager, I worked as a television studio technician at the local municipal center. It was here that I met Karen, a young lady who would play a pivotal role in my life. Have you ever met a genuinely good person? Essentially, I am referring to a person who is pleasant to know, pleasant to be with, and pleasant to be around. Specifically, I am referring to a person whose presence merely enhances your quality of life. Well, Karen was then and remains that kind of person today. Through our tragedies, triumphs, loves, and failed relationships, we maintained a meaningful and healthy friendship.

As the years passed, our friendship progressed and morphed oddly into what had the appearance of a relationship from my perspective but was simply a healthy friendship from hers. I wanted more. But she wanted to pursue her dreams. In a very selfish act, I asked Karen to choose a relationship with me or to let me go. Unselfishly, she honored my request, and we parted ways. Although I initiated the actions that forced her to make this decision, I could not help but feel rejected by her choice.

Essentially, I took her thumbs down as an insult to me rather than seeing it for what it was, another sign that I lacked the maturity and experience needed to be in a relationship.

Look After Love

It was not long before my feelings of rejection turned into anger. I remember saying, "I'll show her! She is going to regret the day she rejected me." As a card-carrying Christian, I knew better than to have feelings of retribution. But as a man, I needed to be justified in my feelings. In hindsight, the feelings of rejection that I experienced were not merely the result of this one perceived relationship failure involving Karen, it was the compound effect of all my failed relationships, and life experiences involving rejection. During my first marriage, I made the mistake of saying "I DO!" before fully comprehending what marriage truly means.

Thus, I entered the union without the benefit of marriage counseling, premarital investigation, wedding planning, or a genuine commitment of honor for myself or the women to whom I would eventually become married. I must admit that our marriage was strictly a matter of convenience for both of us. She sought refuge from unsavory living conditions while I was searching for relief for my high libido and my low self-esteem. Within a few days, I realized I had made a terrible mistake. Suddenly, this marriage of convenience had become increasingly inconvenient, irritating, disrespectful, volatile, and downright irreconcilable, creeping inch by inch toward what would essentially be divorce.

For ten long years, I suffered the consequences of the hell I introduced to my life. Besides the fact that I pledged my soul before God, and all of creation to a woman I did not love, I joined my life and the lives of my immediate family to a woman that I would eventually learn, that I did not like as a human being. Several years after our divorce, I would discover through counseling sessions that my contempt for her had more to do with the intense anger that I had for myself; anger which derived from my not listening to divine wisdom. In retrospect, if I had had a strong knowledge of myself, I would have known that the woman that would become Ex-Wife #1 was not the right one for me.

Put The Word Out

As I said, our marriage was not about loving each other. It was about convenience. There were a number of things in our lives that we were trying to escape. We will discuss those various entities in a moment. But there are two characteristics that stand out more than the rest. She wanted to marry me because she wanted a spouse that would take care of her and her two children. I on the other hand wanted to marry her because I enjoyed our sexual experiences. Yep! I married solely for the sex. I know, I know! It is a dumb reason for getting married. But people do it every day.

In my case, I was in my early twenties. I was too young and stupid to make such an adult decision. During this time of my life, I only cared about two things, what woman I would be dining with for dinner, and where we would have sex after. So, with that said, I made the critical mistake of getting married to a woman simply because I enjoyed her vagina. Although all the red flags and warning signs of our relationship pointed to disaster, I unwisely took her hand in marriage and began the long winding descent into our perfect union in hell.

Again, in hindsight, the warning signs were so evident that the day before we went to stand before the justice of the peace, I told her that I never wanted to see her again—

EVER! However, her request for one last night together tickled my desire for sexual intoxication. Subsequently, I made the worst decision I could ever make in a million lifetimes. Several years and child support payments later, I discovered through counseling reasons for why I made so many unhealthy relationship decisions and believe may have stumbled upon why so many other people do the same.

Narcissistic Personality Disorder

Narcissistic Personality Disorder is a condition in which people have an inflated sense of self-importance and an extreme preoccupation with themselves. A person with a narcissistic personality disorder may:

- React to criticism with anger, shame, or disgrace
- Take advantage of other people to achieve their individual goals
- Have extreme feelings of self-importance
- Exaggerate achievements and abilities
- Preoccupied with fantasies of success, power, beauty, intelligence, or love
- Unreasonable expectations of favorable treatment
- Constant attention and admiration
- Disregard the feelings of others, and have little ability to feel empathy
- Obsessive self-interest
- Follow predominantly selfish goals

Where Did I Go Wrong

There are a variety of things that happen in life that cause people to feel inadequate:

- Low self-esteem
- Weight
- Appearance
- Materialism
- Living Arrangements

- Finances
- Credit
- Education
- Race
- Sickness

Through counseling, I learned that my feelings involving personal failures or inadequacies caused me to specifically seek out women that were needy. I desired women with low self-esteem. In my efforts to become some type of hero in their lives, this allowed me to hide behind my personal frailties and insecurities. I wanted to be the proverbial prince rescuing the damsel in distress. In this way, I was like a crab at the bottom of the ocean, eagerly picking up the pieces of despair. In general, a person who fits into this category will date someone even if the individual has:

- Children
- Character issues
- Anorexia
- Drug Addiction
- Weight Problems

- Low Self-Esteem
- Bad Credit
- Insecurities
- Bad Reputation
- Illness

In my experience, the more complex the problem, the

better. Why is this? By being their hero, I was able to hide from what I needed to fix in my life. If helping a woman through their mess ultimately meant me getting what I wanted out the deal, which was sex and adoration, then that was a win by all accounts for me. In hindsight, I was an absolute fool. When I met the woman that would eventually become Ex-Wife #2, my fears, problems, and narcissistic personality disorder were in overdrive.

All Talked Out

Just a few days after I requested Karen to be with me or to leave me the heck alone, in a small, storefront church, seeds were being planted for what would change my life forever. Essentially, the extensions of a man were about to begin. Have you ever heard the expression; you are what you attract? Well, that is a true statement. If you are a person of standards, morals, and good character, it is likely that you will attract the same. Conversely, if you are a lawless miscreant with low moral standards and a awful personality, expect a similar person to arrive at your doorstep. With Ex-Wife #2, this was my peculiar reality. I attracted a person looking for a way out of their complicated world. Along with being misguided, she was also a bit of a narcissist. Her moral standards were very questionable, and she was easily titillated by the next best thing. Regularly burdened by her unwise decisions, Ex-Wife #2 sought relief in new romances.

Meeting and eventually getting married gave us both the relief we needed from facing the difficult realities of our bad choices, and our broken lives. However, when it became apparent to her that I was no longer a distraction from her problems, but rather a disturbance, a few months after saying "I DO!" she said, "I'm Done!" and just like that, our relationship was over. Man, I called her every expletive that I could call to mind. I damned her for bringing misery into my life. At that time, you could not have told me that I did not love her or that she did not love me. But a decade plus removed, I could see that it was simply about the distractions we offered each other. In hindsight, what made me angry more than anything, was the fact that she grasped the pointlessness of our relationship before I did.

Mind Blowing Decisions

Looking back on both of these relationships, I cannot say that either of them offered me the opportunity to experience happiness. I was as much at odds with them as they were with me. This reminds me of the many famous female stars who are returning to the singles market following a high-profile breakup. In many cases, you will hear men say things like, "She is so fine, I would have done anything to keep her in my bed." Yes, that sounds great from the outside looking in. However, it is possible that the most beautiful face, and the most attractive body, may cause the most pain. Therefore, not all that glitters is gold. Most people continue to date a romantic partner based solely on their sexual attraction, which is indicative of the lust-driven side of humanity, which prefers the material over the spiritual.

As a result of the second marriage's failure, I found myself in a tailspin, from which I did not believe I would be able to recover. Again, I was the common denominator in both of my failed marriages. I was not forced into a relationship by either of these women. As a result, I have to admit that some of the tailspin I experienced was brought on by my own arrogance.

Nevertheless, I was at that crossroads of life you often hear people talk about. In that pivotal moment, an individual chooses to live and move forward or to end his or her life and the suffering they are experiencing. Regardless of which decision is made, the individual is aware that limbo is not an option. If there was ever a time in my life when death seemed more desirable than living, it would have been the days following the end of my marriage to Ex-Wife #2.

People often ask me why I wanted to die after I confessed to not being in love. It was because I felt ashamed, embarrassed, and my ego was bruised. Additionally, I wanted to die because I once again encountered my old friend rejection. It was disappointing that my pastor rejected my request for premarital counseling. After being married without my pastor's counsel, I was rejected by Ex-Wife #2 when she refused to reveal her reasons for ending the marriage. In both instances, I was reminded of experiences with rejection from my school days. As a result, I wanted life to end because I felt that I had been made to look like a fool, and there was no one to blame except myself.

Leavin' For A Dream

I must say, the days leading up to my exit of our apartment were amongst the loneliest, and saddest days of my life. Not since my marriage to Ex-Wife #1 had I felt such a feeling. Being shut down and shunned, without explanation, is something that I have always had a tough time understanding. There I was moving my belongings without as much as a single reason as to why our relationship ended. It has been more than a decade since our demise, and I still do not know. And I am certain that I never will. After storing my personal effects, I went to the only place on earth where I knew I could find peace. I went home to my parents. After I explained what had happened to them both, they both assured me that things would get better. Moreover, they stressed very emphatically the importance of learning from my mistakes and moving forward. After experiencing the difficult emotions associated with low self-esteem and rejection, I yelled at the top of my voice, "Why do people I love continue to walk away from my life?"

Within seconds, a voice spoke to me and said, "Now you know how I feel when people break covenant with me, turn from me, and I have done nothing wrong!" As soon as I heard those words in my spirit, I knew that the hurtful feeling I had experienced in both failed relationships was what I was doing in my relationship with my Creator. I had neglected the divine relationship with the entity that spared my life and enabled me to overcome cancer, in pursuit of what made me feel good.

Immediately, I realized what I had done wrong. It was unwise of me to allow distractions of life to become my gods. Therefore, chasing these things was the errant focus of my life:

- Vanity
- Wardrobe
- Consumerism
- Television
- Entertainment
- Alcohol
- Gluttony

- Image
- Romance
- Sex
- Money
- Status
- Career
- Power & Influence

It took quite some time for me to get past the hurt and pain of that experience. I had to put in some hard work to get my life back on track.

Although it was difficult, I was determined that my life and my decisions in the future would be different than before. Aside from this, I resolved to build new relationships based on my mature self rather than the broken and self-abused man I had become from neglect. As a result of this rebirth of sorts, I made a conscious effort to rebuild the friendships that had been damaged by my calloused behavior. Having said that, the first apology I made was to Karen.

After separating and eventually divorcing Ex-Wife #2, I learned through counseling that I could not expect others to sacrifice their dreams, goals, and aspirations for my purposes. In light of that, I decided to call Karen. Having hurt her, I prepared myself to be chastised. The rejection I felt caused me to say some things that caused her a lot of harm. Although she could have blown me off and told me to kill myself, she forgave me.

Her kindness played a tremendous role in helping me through my darkest hour simply because she forgave me and allowed our friendship to be renewed. In the years that followed, I was able to piece my life together in a way that I can look and the mirror and be proud of what I have become as a person, a human being, and a child of light. This episode of my life taught me what it means to be honorable, and certainly, what it means to be honored.

Fortunately, I was able to make it through this experience with my life. There are a number of people that are so overcome by the weight of relationship failure, that they end it all, and take their own lives. I am so glad that life afforded me a second chance. As a result, I devote much of my time these days to guiding people through the unfortunate realities of relationships and the mishaps that occur very often.

Today, I am living the dream. After journeying through a period of learning myself, and getting to know me, I met someone, fell in love, and eventually married. In fact, we have been by each other's side for more than a decade. As for Karen, well she eventually found love too. I am happy to say that not only are we still best friends after all of these years, but she is also my wife. So, if you are one of those people that believe finding your one true love is impossible. I am a living testimony to the reality that all things are possible. Although I had used the word "honor" many times before, I never understood what it was like to honor someone or be honored until life gave me Karen.

Always and Forever

When we decided to get married, we declared that divorce would never again be an option for either of us. During the entire time we dated, we never had sexual intercourse, or sex of any variety. There was no rubbing, tongue kissing, or touching. In fact, we never came close, and it was never an issue. How were we able to accomplish this? Well, it is because we kept our eyes focused to the larger picture, that being our friendship and our desire to give our relationship the room that it needed to grow and the respect it deserved. In short, not screwing around gave us the guarantee of not screwing up.

It allowed us to spend twenty weeks in marriage counseling, digging deep to find out everything we needed to learn about ourselves, each other, family history, finances, credit, likes, dislikes, joys, pains, distresses, and other matters. It also afforded us the time needed to take blood tests to see if either of us was infected with HIV/AIDS or other diseases that could negatively impact our marriage. Additionally, it gave us time to allow our parents and children to become adjusted to the idea of a new blended family.

Doing it right afforded all of us the chance to enjoy what we are experiencing now, and that my friend, is the joy, happiness, and peace of a loving and happy family. The happiness that we are experiencing can only occur when two people decide to live a principled life. And it is through that discipline and determination that one can experience a wonderful relationship. In my wildest dreams, I would have never thought that my winding road of bad relationships would have led me to where I am at this point in my life today.

Likewise, I would have never thought it possible to find a life partner as compatible as I have seen in my wife. With that said, if life afforded me the opportunity to overcome the challenges of all my dysfunctions, inadequacies, and failures, to allow me to experience a great marriage, you can do it also. But in order to do it, you must commit the entirety of your being to the following efforts:

- You should be honest with yourself and other people about who you are as a person.

- Identify and correct those aspects of your character that require improvement.

- Identify the attributes about you that make you valuable to a relationship.

- Find out what makes you a weakness or a liability.

- Determine the purpose for which you are seeking a relationship.

- Besides your sex, smile, body, and physical attributes, what do you bring to a relationship?

- Are you willing to research, investigate, and evaluate the background of your potential spouse? Likewise, are you willing to allow them to do the same?

- On the basis of the evidence presented, can you decide whether to commit to a relationship or whether to disengage?

- Are you able to uphold your commitments?

If you are capable of doing these things, then I am certain that you can have the type of relationship that you desire to have. If you cannot do these things, then I am equally certain that you will not have the relationship that you desire but you will indeed experience the relationship you deserve. Those that attend class, but do not study tend to fail class or that the very least, get scores that are unfavorable. They get these grades because they deserve them. When it comes to your relationship, your family, children, unborn children, and even your ancestors are counting on you to make the right decisions.

Never lose sight of this reality, no matter how big the bulge may be in his pants, or how large the breast might appear in her halter top. Always keep your eyes focus to what matters and ignore those aspects of life that our fleeting. Remember, when it comes to relationships and what is critically important for your life, and happiness, you are the star of the story, not all of that other stuff.

CHAPTER 1 | **DEEP FACTS & TAKEAWAYS**

1) According to the latest data available, the marriage rate in the United States was 6.1 per 1,000 people.

2) Divorces in the U.S. were 2.7 per 1,000 in 2007 (44 states and D.C. reported). This is known as the "crude divorce rate." The crude divorce rate can be used to describe changes in divorce rates over time, but it does not provide accurate information on the proportion of first marriages that end in divorce.

3) There is a decrease in both marriage rates and divorce rates in the United States as of 2019, with the marriage rate dropping from 8.2 to 6.1 per 1,000 people in 2000 and the divorce rate from 4.0 to 2.7. A number of studies have shown that millennials are choosing to wait longer to get married and stay married longer and are responsible for the decline in both marriage and divorce rates in the US.

RELATIONSHIP IQ | **INSIGHTFUL QUESTIONS**

- What excites you about marriage?
- What scares you about marriage?
- What does having a "life" outside of "us" mean to you?
- How do you propose a couple "grows together?"

- What does romance mean to you? What do you consider romantic?

- What does "through thick and thin till the end" mean to you?

- Do you see yourself feeling content with marriage and family life?

- If certain aspects of either one makes you nervous or uncomfortable, why?

- In what areas are you willing to compromise to maintain a healthy and balanced marriage?

"By wisdom a house is built, and by understanding it is established; by knowledge the rooms are filled with all precious and pleasant riches. A wise man is full of strength, and a man of knowledge enhances his might, for by wise guidance you can wage your war, and in abundance of counselors there is victory."

Proverbs 24:3-6

Chapter

2

Building For A Successful Marriage

I t has been thought by biblical scholars that lust has played a fundamental role in the destruction and early termination of all relationships since the fall of humanity in the Garden of Eden. It is responsible for the destruction of nations, it has laid waste to politicians, preachers, members of the clergy, and, yes, it has even destroyed the marriages of those once hopelessly in love. Wouldn't it be nice if there were some foolproof systems that could ensure that people considering marriage have a future as stable as the roads and bridges, we cross on our way to work every day? Such a system exists, and it is based squarely on sacred history and scripture. To benefit from these principles, however, you must be willing to embrace The Creator's teachings, wisdom, and wise counsel. In the Holy Bible's book of Hosea, Chapter 4, verse six says:

"My people are destroyed for lack of knowledge: because thou hast rejected knowledge, I will also reject thee, that thou shalt be no priest to me: seeing thou hast forgotten the law of thy God, I will also forget thy children."

Throughout each aspect of our lives and especially in our intimate relationships, our Creator is expected to be at the center of all we do. Our goal should be to learn and apply wisdom to combat bad actors and the enemies of humanity. The light of wisdom has led us out of the dark ages and into the marvelous present. It is foolishness that leads people to reject Wisdom, for they follow folly instead of the counsel of our Creator's goodness and mercy. We cannot expect to succeed in any of our plans or activities if we do not embrace knowledge, wisdom, and the true power of our Creator that encompasses us.

In the Holy Bible's book of Proverbs, Chapter 4, verse seven says, "Wisdom is the principal thing; therefore get wisdom: and with all thy getting get understanding." What does this mean for you and me?

If we expect to receive the correct answers to life's bewildering questions, we should have wisdom in our toolbox to tackle those difficult questions when they arise. Consequently, when the text says, "...and with all thy getting get understanding.", it is telling us that merely thinking that we know the answer or hoping to know it will not suffice; we must know the answer, or we will be doomed to failure. Unfortunately, most people cannot obtain divine wisdom through direct means because of many intentional distractions. We are subject to various distractions that interfere with the communication between our human minds, our intellectual design, and the frequencies that connect these properties. That being said, most people are confined to stories that are derived from sacred texts, as told by different individuals during religious gatherings. However, if we are honest, we realize that an individual cannot survive solely on the words of another. Divine wisdom, knowledge, and instruction must be harvested and applied by oneself to one's heart before it can take root in that individual. As many of our top athletes can attest, they do not become the best in the world by simply watching and copying the work of their predecessors. As a result, they put in the extra hours of effort to improve themselves and become better. As part of their training program, they exercise, eat well, and maintain a healthy lifestyle in order to achieve optimum performance. While training, if the athlete reaches a plateau of sorts, a coach might be heard saying "Come on, dig deeper and give me one more." In a similar manner, the Creator is encouraging us to do just that. As we struggle with life's challenges, as we deal with life's circumstances, God is the coach, urging us to dig deep and be our best selves. But if your life is devoid of substance, you can dig for eternity, and you will never find the answers you need to cope with life's challenges.

Throughout mankind's wisdom, there is a great deal of conflict and contradiction. In the soil of the Creator, you will find knowledge and wisdom beyond your wildest imaginations. Having said that, marriage and a desire to spend the rest of your life with someone are not just about knowing what you want, they are also about using wisdom, knowledge, and The Creator to guide you. Be sure to do your homework before diving into anything. But especially a romance.

Have faith but also arm yourself with the fundamental principles needed to move all things from a concealed status to revealed, as this will allow you to make decisions based on facts or what is known rather than simply hoping for the best or a positive outcome. In my view, when attempting to determine whether marriage to a person is a good or bad idea, there are three fundamental steps one should use to obtain the answers needed. The steps involve research, investigation, and evaluation. Let us take a look at each of them and explore their rich meanings.

Research	Diligent and systematic inquiry or investigation into a subject in order to discover or revise facts, theories, applications, etc.
Investigation	A detailed inquiry, systematic examination, or careful search or examination to discover facts.
Evaluation	A systematic determination of merit, worth, and significance of something or someone using criteria against a set of standards.

In short, research, investigation, and evaluation all mean that we have a responsibility to dig deep before we leap into marriage. So, why are the steps of research, investigation, and evaluation so important? Have you ever been in a relationship or involved with a person who was definitely unstable? If you have not, it is possible that the unstable person is you. All kidding aside, the role that stability plays in a healthy relationship cannot be understated.

To understand the role stability plays in relationships, we first have to understand its meaning. Stability derives from the word "stable," which means:

- Unwavering

- Sane or mentally sound

- Dependable

- Not subject to emotional instability or illness

- Not changeable, as in character or purpose

Therefore, before you change your relationship status from "single" to "married" on your social network pages, it is important that you first determine whether both you and your partner are unwavering in mind, body, and spirit. If we eliminate the couples that want to get married for reasons other than love, I think the vast majority of people who get married do so with the understanding that this is indeed a lifetime commitment.

Considering this, I think that it would be worthwhile to find out whether there were any psychological or mental health challenges involved. An acquaintance of mine discovered their spouse had psychological issues after several years of marriage. This revelation was absolutely devastating, and it eventually wrecked their marriage. As a matter of fact, I think we can all agree that five years into a relationship with children, pets, and financial obligations, it is not an appropriate time to learn that one is married to an individual that is unhinged.

Emotional Instability

Instability can be classified in a variety of ways. Insanity is the most extreme form of mental illness, but emotional instability in my view is a close second. If you are considering marrying an emotionally unstable individual, and you have never been counseled, trained, or have any information about what this journey will be like with this person, then it might be a wise decision to have your own head examined to determine if you are mentally healthy. As a general rule, I believe emotionally unstable people are not completely bonkers, but they are frightening enough to warrant concern.

Emotionally unstable people tend to behave in an unpredictable, erratic, and alarming manner. A bit unpredictable? A bit erratic? Is it really worth getting romantically involved with someone who is emotionally unpredictable or erratic? Most of us would probably respond, "No way!" Unfortunately, what most of us say and what we often do are two different things. Today, many people have broken relationships or unhappy marriages simply because they ignored the warning signs, or plainly stated, red flags of emotional instability.

Clear Signs of Emotional Instability

a. Relationships with others are intense but stormy and unstable, with marked shifts in feelings and difficulty maintaining intimate, close connections.

b. Person may manipulate others and often has difficulty trusting others.

c. Feelings of emptiness.

d. Depression.

e. Irritability.

f. Anxiety.

g. Unpredictable and impulsive behavior, which might include excessive spending, promiscuity, gambling, drug or alcohol abuse, shoplifting, overeating, or physically self-damaging actions such as suicide gestures.

h. Inappropriate and intense anger or rage with temper tantrums, constant brooding and resentment, feelings of deprivation, and a loss of control or fear of loss of control over angry feelings.

i.   Disturbance, confusion, and uncertainty about self-identity, sexuality, life goals and values, career choices, and friendships.

j.   Deep-seated feeling that one is flawed, defective, damaged, or bad in some way, with a tendency to go to extremes in thinking, feeling, or behavior.

k.   Under extreme stress or in severe cases, there can be brief psychotic episodes with loss of contact with reality or bizarre behavior or symptoms.

l.   Even in less severe instances, there is often significant disruption of relationships and work performance.

Typically, these relationships involve individuals who have an arrogant sense of self-importance, believing they can shape others into what they desire in an attempt to produce the ideal spouse or submissive partner. These very emotionally unstable relationships thrive on elements of control and tend not to end well. In fact, these types of relationships typically turn volatile and can sometimes lead to near death encounters.

In the fall of 2005, the nation learned about a woman named Yvette Cade, a domestic violence survivor that suffered burns to nearly 70% of her body when her estranged husband showed up to her place of employment, doused her with gasoline and set her on fire. Several years and surgeries later, Cade not only deals with the physical scars from her attack, but she also must live with the mental and emotional scars caused by her now ex-husband.

And speaking of the ex-husband, unless paroled he will spend the rest of his natural life behind bars contemplating the very selfish and almost deadly choice, he made that day. People contemplating marriage to a possibly emotionally unstable person should consider situations like that of Yvette Cade. If you have not begun asking questions about your spouse's mental history or the family's mental history, it is a good idea to start now.

Also, if you are involved with someone who consistently exhibits any of the twelve signs of emotional instability, you really should be asking yourself the question, "Of the hundreds of millions of people on this planet that I can choose from to be my spouse, is this one person really worth the risk?" Why should we involve our futures, our families, and the potential lives of unborn children and ourselves with someone who clearly has issues? Would you try to hang a picture on a wall that was clearly unstable? Would you attempt to build a home on a weak foundation? In light of these examples, why would we involve ourselves with people who are equally unstable?

Steadfast

If you are considering marriage to your potential significant other, you should do only so if both you and your potential mate are steadfast people. The word steadfast means fixed in place, immovable, not subject to change, dutifully firm and unwavering. This is an important attribute for all relationships that hold any redeemable value whatsoever. However, in the marriage relationship, this attribute is paramount. People with this attribute are loyal, committed, and dedicated to the principles and ideals of marriage.

Steadfast couples are serious about their marriage vows, particularly the vows that speak to for better, for worse, for richer, for poorer, in sickness, and in health. These couples delight in the good and troubled times simply because they delight in each other and allow the creator to light their path. Typically, these are the types of couples that work together as a unit and for the greater good of their marriage. In other words, no outside force or entity, not even sickness or death, can separate the bond shared between the two.

Couples of this nature are determined not to let any situation stand in the way of their love, no matter how difficult it may seem. You should certainly look for this kind of character trait in your spouse, and you should also seek it out in yourself. Matches that are most appropriate to your preferences should more often than not reflect your own personality. In other words, if you are an emotionally unstable person, you should expect another emotionally unstable person to gravitate towards you. By focusing on improving your emotional, spiritual, and mental well-being, you will be able to attract the right person to your space in the universe.

Communication

Many people are in unhappy marriages simply because they failed to perform an in-depth self-evaluation before marriage. Second, they failed to investigate the person they were marrying and, finally, they failed to study and understand the principles of what constitutes a God-filled marriage. Unfortunately, the similarity that many of these bad marriages share revolves around the fact that there was probably more premarital penetration (sex) in the beginning of the relationship than there was real, deep human-to-human communication.

After my second marriage crashed and burned, I went into a deep, dark depression. I went through the doldrums of despair because I simply could not figure out what went wrong. After several months of soul-searching, I have finally discovered the source of my error. I put physical inclinations before effective communication. Ultimately, this resulted in what would be a second failed marriage. Very simply, I knew nothing about the woman I married, and she knew nothing about me. Because of our failure to communicate truthfully to one another, we both ended up with this huge mistake on our records.

Communication is, without a doubt, the single most important focus couples must have if their relationship is to have the slightest chance of success. It is indeed the glue that binds all human relationships together. The communication focus is vitally important for the development of all relationships, but it is critically important for the success of the marital relationship, for no one other than God will ever be as close to you as your spouse.

Through all the good, bad, and indifferent times you will have in life and your relationship, your ability to communicate effectively and positively through all of life's extremes will make the difference. Therefore, it is important to always keep the lines of communication open and never stop talking to one another. In the initial stages of a relationship, when people are just getting to know each other, there is a lot of topical or surface conversation. However, if you are considering marriage to someone, you need to be in the caverns of conversation; this means that your talks should be in-depth.

In your conversations, you should be digging for more than simply knowing what your mate's favorite ice cream is; you should be digging deep to discover whether ice cream gives them gas. In addition, while on the subject of gas, couples who find their marriages out of gas do so partly because they forgot to talk to one another and began talking at each other.

If you are considering marriage today, ask yourself the question, "How is our communication?" If your answer is, "It can be better," my suggestion is that you work on the "better" before saying, "I DO!" If you are not building a bridge of communication that allows you to open up, talk, share, and express yourself from the depths of your heart, then you are building a bridge to nowhere.

Guys, before you take the ring back to the jewelers, understand that you and your potential spouse may not always see things eye to eye. Your conversations may not always be ones to write home to momma about—but that is ok.

People do not always agree or see eye to eye. However, when you are able to keep the lines of communication open, focused on that positive place that says that, whether we agree, disagree, or agree to disagree, I love you and I am not leaving, then you can achieve marital success. I cannot stress enough the immense importance and value of effective, clear, focused, positive, and loving communication. Successful married couples learn how to communicate through their differences, for the goal is to maintain and sustain a place in unity–that is the place where wedded couples find their bliss.

CHAPTER 2 | **DEEP FACTS & TAKEAWAYS**

1. In America, a divorce occurs every 42 seconds. This is equal to 86 divorces per hour, 2,046 divorces per day, 14,364 divorces per week, and 746,971 divorces per year.

2. Approximately every 16 seconds, there is a marriage in the United States. This equates to 230 marriages per hour, 38,762 marriages per week, and 2,015,603 marriages per year.

3. During the time it takes for a couple to recite their vows (2 minutes), nearly 3 divorces occur.

4. Nearly 172 divorces happen during a typical romantic comedy movie (2 hours).

5. On average, 430 divorces occur during a wedding reception (5 hours).

RELATIONSHIP IQ | **INSIGHTFUL QUESTIONS**

- What would you do if one of us became addicted to a substance?

- If we were having relationship problems, would you be open to work with a counselor?

- Do you consider yourself a jealous person? How do you handle this?

- Is getting married seen as a mandatory goal that you must achieve in life?

- Name a couple that you know who have a great marriage. What attributes of their marriage would you like to emulate?

And let the peace that comes from Christ rule in your hearts. For as members of one body you are called to live in peace. And always be thankful."

Colossians 3:15

Chapter

3

IDENTIFYING A POTENTIAL SPOUSE ABUSER

I f you travel down any road in the world, you will see signs or signals that draw attention to a particular warning or caution. There are yellow signs that warn you to proceed with caution, green signs that tell you when to move forward, and red signs that tell you when to stop. As it relates to signs and relationships, I want to focus your attention on the red signs or warning signals that tell us when to stop. Have you noticed that most of the technology we use today comes equipped with built-in warning signals? For example, our cars have signals that warn us if our safety belts are loose or if the door is ajar. Our mobile devices have alarms to tell us when our batteries are running low, and even our landline telephones have signals that tell us when another call is on the line. These built-in warning systems are called telltale signs.

These signs or warnings are indicators that tell the status of a situation within a particular mechanism or system. Like the technology we use every day, relationships also have built-in telltale signs that provide us with warnings we need regarding possible relationship problems. In the world of relationships, we call these telltale signs "red flags." A red flag can be any undesirable characteristic that stands out. Most divorcees will tell you that the red flag warning signs were there before marriage, but for whatever reason, they chose to ignore them, thus ending up in the divorce line. Typically, these marital disasters can be avoided when relationship deal-breakers are predefined before entering into a relationship.

So, you're probably asking, "What are relationship deal-breakers?" Well, these are predefined situations that would immediately give pause to an out-of-bounds condition. For example, say you are at a local restaurant, and you notice the cook wiping his nose while preparing your food. Would you eat it? If your answer is no, that's likely because you have specific rules that do not allow for nose picking while preparing your meals. In relationships, the principle for predefined out-of-bounds conditions is essentially the same. As an individual, you should have some predefined standards that are simply uncompromising. So, if you are seriously talking about marriage, you may want to create some guiding principles that involve your role in your marital relationship. Moreover, these predetermined standards should be tied to your list of red flag conditions.

So, with that said, do you have any predefined values attached to your relationship? If so, what are they? Also, can you recognize the red flags associated with these predefined principles? If you haven't had the opportunity to develop a list of the predefined tenets, now is the time to do so. It is imperative to remember that these are not fabricated reasons for ending a relationship. But rather tools to keep you from losing perspective while dating. Essentially, tools purposed to save your life. As we discussed in Chapter 2, Yvette Cade suffered burns to nearly 70% of her body as a result of the abusive husband she had the unfortunate experience of marrying. Because of events like these, recognizing early warning signs are absolutely essential.

Life can sometimes be challenging and complex. Sometimes, people with the warmest personality snap and lose it. Sadly, in these moments, people of good character make poor decisions. In the wake of those decisions are the lives shattered by a choice.

It can be as simple as not putting on your seatbelt and getting pulled over for a ticket. Or something significant like drinking and driving and causing a fatal accident. No one ever sets out to create these dire situations. But bad decisions lead to bad situations happening. So, if you're considering marriage, you need to make sure that you are not compromising your predefined principles to be in a relationship. Women and men find themselves involved with people they would never have expected. However, a lapse in judgement caused them to be connected with a person that would alter their being. Although Ms. Cade and her ex-husband are no longer married, they will always be linked together because of this horrific incident. So, for marriage, you should establish some predefined principles that pertain to abuse.

Now there are four common types of abuse:

- Physical
- Verbal
- Mental
- Emotional

The risk of being involved in an abusive relationship is likely if you don't know what red flags to avoid. There are obvious red flags such as anger, passiveness, jealousy, violence, and controlling behavior. Unfortunately, most abusers hide their true nature while dating. Hence, the true identity of an individual or, more accurately, the monster within emerges after an individual has become attached, or at worst after they have exchanged wedding vows. Based on this reality, some real telltale signs (i.e., red flags, warnings, etc.) will alert you to a potential abuser. When you see any of these attributes, attitudes, or behaviors displayed by someone, run like hell. These warning signs can be detected before a relationship is formed and before accepting or offering a marriage proposal.

Eight Warning Signs of a Potential Abusive Relationship

If you observe or personally experience any of the following characteristics on display, you may be in a relationship with an abuser:

- Always Placing Blame
- Refuse to Accept responsibility
- Collector of Injustices
- Frequently Angry
- Their way or else
- Superiority Complex
- Argumentative
- Very Cynical & Sarcastic
- Jealous Behavior
- Practitioner of Deception

Blame Game

Generally, these individuals tend to blame their problems in life on other people or circumstances that have nothing to do with them. These are the types of people who, in brand-new relationships, will hold you up as the hero, while portraying an ex-lover as the villain. As an example, you might hear something like, "You are so caring, sweet, and loving. You are not like that jerk I was with before." Or, "I wish I had met you before I got involved with that maniac." In this type of circumstance, their praise serves primarily to persuade you that all they really require is a bit of love and care. They believe that somehow, they are misunderstood, mischaracterized, victimized, and that no one else understands them but you.

But in reality, this is far from the truth. Rather than a relationship, they need psychological treatment to help them resolve their unresolved issues. Lastly, most blamers view themselves as victims. Essentially, they have a victim's mentality. That is to say, they are always the ones who are victimized. Accordingly, they justify many of their errant behaviors and selfish actions. In light of this, you need to pay close attention and be aware of the red flags and warning signs.

Bitterness

The second red flag warning sign involves the area of past relationships known as bitterness. When you hear the word bitterness, what do you think of it? When I hear the word, I often think of the baggage one tends to carry from relationship to relationship that gets heavier and heavier over time, causing many people to lash out ruthlessly against a person because of the compound effect of several others. Whichever way you slice it, bitterness is a funky attitude caused by one person's perception of their reality and their inability to let this said reality go. Also, bitter people tend to see the things that have to happen to them as wrong or unfair. They also tend to believe that they are not getting enough attention, love, affection, praise, and recognition. Thus, bitter people live in a perpetual state of bitterness that they lose sight of any reality than their own.

Unfortunately, this often leads to someone being victimized or abused out of displaced anger or emotion perpetrated by the embittered lover. So, if you decide to marry a person who has a bit of a bitter streak, you are more likely to become a part of what makes up their sad existence, thereby possibly becoming the focal point of their anger.

Privilege

Third, on our list of red flag warning signs is the area of privilege. Have you ever met a person that believes the world should cater to them? As a result, you understand precisely what I mean when I use the word privilege. How does that relate to abuse? People who believe they are entitled to special treatment, consideration, or attention tend to be rude and self-serving. There is no concern for anyone other than themselves. A typical example of these individuals would be someone who would sell out their mother in order to save their skin. This trend is becoming more prevalent in our society. We see it on the crowded subway ride home when a man refuses to sacrifice his comfort to allow a woman and her child to have his seat.

At the local shopping centers, we often see this happen when someone aggressively pulls into a parking space. All the time pretending they did not notice the person preparing to back into the open space. It happens daily in our legal system when privileged people are sentenced to 30 months, while those who are not privileged are sentenced to 30 years. Yes, privilege is a real danger in the mind of an offender because it means they believe:

- It's my right to rape someone if I want.
- I can victimize people as I want
- And I certainly can murder them wherever I wish and dump their corpses in the river if I desire.

Without a doubt, this is the mindset of a privileged offender. I consider this to be a clear and present danger for the individual with whom they are in contact.

Superiority Complex

Typically, this is an attribute that is synonymous with men. However, this behavior is not exclusive to the male franchise. A person who meets this characteristic has an inflated sense of self and feels the need to point out why they are the best, brightest, and most brilliant.

These are folks that "lord" over others meaning they have a sense of power and authority. This is one of the most abusive red flag areas of concern. When people operate from this mindset, they see others as being beneath their level. In other words, in their world, the hierarchy of importance may look something like this:

Hierarchy of Importance

1. Money
2. Food
3. House
4. Dog
5. Automobile
6. Clothes
7. Sports
8. Job
9. Friends
10. You

Lastly, when a person has a superiority complex, they expect you to surrender your mind, independence of thought, and sensibility for what's right over to their way of thinking. Therefore, if you're found in non-compliance, you will suffer the wrath and full consequences of what they deem to be disrespectful behavior. If you find yourself in a relationship where you feel undervalued, or your opinion is not considered, this is a red flag sign that you may be involved with an abuser.

Quarrelsome

If you are involved with someone that is generally argumentative, you are probably dating an individual that makes a big deal out of unimportant things and commonly finds fault with everything. Typically, this is a person that can be very petty-minded. This characteristic often leads to mental and emotional abuse and will undoubtedly take a physical toll on one's body over time. In a relationship like this, the flying expletives and verbal assaults will diminish your spirit and demoralize your character if you allow yourself to become involved in this type of relationship. Again, there are more than a billion people on the planet. Why spend your valuable life with a complete knucklehead?

Cynicism and Sarcasm

Typically, these egomaniacs garner pleasure by saying harsh and cruel things out of their mouths. Sometimes the things they say are intended to be funny but most times, what they say is downright hurtful. In relationships with people like this, comments are often made about people outside the relationship. However, after marriage, those same hateful and cruel statements will be made about you. Lastly, these are the types of people that will not hesitate to demoralize you in public, in front of family members, friends, or others of high standing. Again, much like the quarrelsome attribute, this characteristic often leads to mental and emotional abuse.

Lies and Deceit

Are you dating a habitual liar? How do you know that you're not if your answer is no? How do you know that the person you're dating is who they say they are? In this age of identity theft, social media, fake identification, and hidden agendas, how can you be sure you're dating who you think you're dating. Have we ever seen or heard of a situation where a person was married to different people in different states at the same time? What about men who found out their lovely bride was a former prostitute after marriage, or what about the women who discovered their husband was gay. How would you like to be a part of that sexual experience? Can you say HIV/AIDS? So, if you start discovering a pattern of deceitfulness, this is a red flag warning sign that will save your life.

Jealousy

This one will get you killed. Ladies, there are many women sprawled out in graveyards because of this attribute. Likewise, there are a lot of men laid out beside them. If you start noticing signs of possessiveness or issues that indicate your partner is becoming a bit controlling, you better pump the breaks and slow that relationship down. At first, it might seem cute. But jealousy is no laughing matter. You have no idea who or what you are dealing with in this crazy age. Seriously, there are many of what I like to call "Band-Aid" people moving about. These individuals are hurt, broken, angry, and cut off from the world. They often are beset with a lot of deep-seated frustrations and irrational thoughts. With that said, please note that playing with a person's emotions could have unsavory consequences.

Some women are DEAD because the person they were with or married to thought they were involved with another man when they weren't. I believe that the most serious and dangerous forms of violence in relationships are born out of this characteristic. So, if you see any sign of these activities whatsoever, have a conversation, keep a watchful eye and be very mindful of the risk.

Red Flags That Point to Other Possible Concerns

- Ill-mannered.
- They are consistently tardy.
- They belittle their family members.
- They obsess over money; they are very materialistic.
- They refer to exes in a derogatory manner (i.e., whores, etc.).
- All their bad relationships were the other person's fault and not theirs.
- Their relationships never last longer than a couple of months.
- They have been married and divorced more than once.
- You have a strong suspicion they are hiding something.
- They frequently ask to borrow money.
- They live with their parents.
- Never-ending drama fills their lives.
- They put down your opinions.
- They openly admit to being unfaithful.
- Nothing is ever good enough.

Red Flags That Can Point To Abuse

- When you are with your partner, does he or she act differently when he or she is with others?
- Is your partner threatening to kill you if you break up with them?

- Do you feel forced to have sex with your partner?

- Does your partner threaten to harm you, your friends, or your family members?

- Is your partner reading your mail or looking through your personal effects?

If you are indeed considering marriage, you should know that communication and observation would do more in helping you to make the right decision regarding marriage than any other investigation tool available. Have you heard the saying "if you give a person enough rope, they will hang themselves?"

Your communication and observation of your potential spouse will do just that. If there are any hidden tendencies, bad habits, or other masked unscrupulous behaviors, your continued communication and observation will uncover the hidden truth. Now, once it is revealed, what will you do with it? Will you ignore it, proceed with getting married, and regret your decision later? Or, will you accept the truth and make the decisions necessary to preserve your well-being?

CHAPTER 3 | **DEEP FACTS & TAKEAWAYS**

1. On average, 5,975,768 marriages end in divorce during the first 8 years of marriage.

2. Over the course of a 40-year period, 67 percent of first marriages end in divorce.

3. A quarter of all Americans 18 years of age or older, regardless of whether they have been married or not, have experienced a divorce.

4. In the United States, fifteen percent of adult women are divorced or separated, compared with less than one percent in 1920.

5. Most first marriages end in divorce after eight years on average.

RELATIONSHIP IQ | **INSIGHTFUL QUESTIONS**

- Were you jealous of some of your friends while growing up? If so, how, and why?

- Would you describe yourself as "popular" in school?

- Were you a late bloomer or forced to mature faster than others while growing up?

- Describe an unpleasant childhood memory that still bothers you.

- Describe a pleasant childhood memory that made an impact on your life.

- Would you like to relive your childhood? Why or why not?

- Describe your first childhood crush.

- Were you picked on as a child? Did you pick on others?

- When you were a child, what role did you play in your household?

"Wives, submit to your own husbands, as to the Lord. For the husband is the head of the wife, even as Christ is the head of the church, his body, and is himself its Savior. Now as the church submits to Christ, so also wives should submit in everything to their husbands. Husbands, love your wives, as Christ loved the church and gave himself up for her, that he might sanctify her, having cleansed her by the washing of water with the word... "

Ephesians 5:22-33

Chapter

4

CHOOSING YOUR FOREVER PARTNER

When we stop and think of people who our society considers genuine winners, we often think of world-class athletes, coaches, and storied sports franchises. However, we know that every segment of society produces winners. The unfortunate thing about winning is that, for someone to win, someone else has to lose. It is simply the natural order of things. In life, sometimes you are the bug, and other times, you are the windshield. In the jungle, there are days when the gazelle is the meal that escapes. However, when the lions are hungry, the gazelle becomes their main dish. Again, somebody has to win, and somebody has to lose. The good news is that everyone can be a winner when selecting the right partner for a relationship. The individuals involved simply need to have a mindset for winning.

Winning Takes Commitment

I remember being selected last to be on any team put together during gym class through grade school. Nothing about my physique suggested that I showed any signs of athleticism. In fact, my body type said just the opposite. From this schoolyard reality, I learned a precious lesson; no one wants to be a part of a losing team. Additionally, no one wants to select an individual for a team that does not offer the best possible chance of winning. All walks of life apply this mindset, except when choosing the best potential spouse. Why is that? There's so much more to choose from, so why are we settling for so little in relationships? I am not speaking from a materialistic or superficial perspective because I believe those types of shallow, transparent relationships never work.

I am talking about people who have entered into marital relationships full of regret because they settled for the next best thing rather than settling for nothing less than what they really and truly wanted. Winners never settle for losing; they never settle for second place. A winner's mindset is to dominate and achieve victory at all costs. This is the type of mindset you must have when deciding whether a person is indeed the right one for you or not. It would be best if you were as selective in choosing your spouse as my schoolmates were with me on the playground.

If you see anything that indicates that the person does not offer you the best possible chance at marital success, you should run like hell until you identify the right person. We should be looking for and seeing clear, distinct characteristics that separate the best possible candidates for marriage from all the rest. One of the most straightforward and apparent attributes to identify involves personal responsibility. Before you consider marriage to anyone, you should be looking to see if they are fully capable of handling their own business.

To determine whether a person has the attributes or characteristics of personal responsibility, you should be digging to discover the following:

- Do they have a job or own their own business?
- Are they financially independent?
- Do they appear to be in debt and strapped for cash?

- Are they currently purchasing their own home, or do they live in an apartment?

- Do they live with their parents? If so, why?

- Do they own a vehicle? If not, why?

Remember, a part of picking the right team means that you have to select the best people as teammates. A "no" response to these questions does not necessarily disqualify a person from being a possible candidate. Still, it certainly indicates that more investigation of this person is needed before a proposal is given or accepted.

Divorce Avoided

For some people, asking these questions may seem a bit intrusive. However, such questions will save you a lot of hassle, heartache, financial loss, and eventual heartbreak. In the U.S. alone, it is estimated that 50% of all marriages end in divorce, with first marriages lasting only about eight years.

Why are people divorcing in the United States?

According to a recent national survey, the most common reason for divorce is a lack of commitment. Below are the reasons and their percentages:

- Lack of commitment 73%

- Argue too much 56%

- Infidelity 55%

- Married too young 46%

- Unrealistic expectations 45%
- Lack of equality in the relationship 44%
- Lack of preparation for marriage 41%
- Domestic Violence or Abuse 25%

—Source: U.S. Census Bureau

If you are considering marriage and want to do it the right way the first time, it behooves you to research, investigate, and evaluate the person you are considering spending the rest of your life with. When people decide to jump the broom, they often think only of the feel-good factors and not the real-life factors that figure into the success or failure of a marriage. In my first attempt at marriage, I focused on the "happily" rather than the "ever after." In essence, I invested my time and attention only in the things that made me feel good in the short term and ignored the things that would ultimately affect my long-term relationship.

Regrettably, my life of bliss eventually turned to misery and sadness as the things I ignored came back to hurt me in a real way. A person can only hide the true essence of who they are for so long. Good or bad, the nature of every man or woman will be revealed and made known for the entire world to see. During the courtship period of a relationship, you have the opportunity to evaluate the person you are dating and determining if they are the person matched for you or someone else.

Researching the background of the person you are

considering marriage to does not make you a bad person; it makes you a hero. When you decide to get married, you ask your family, friends, and children to buy into your vision and dream of happiness. Therefore, you are responsible for ensuring you are not selling them a pipe dream or a bag full of rotten goods. It is unfair to bring people into our lives, create collaborative relationships, and then ask them directly or indirectly to choose sides once the relationship has gone sour.

Another intangible of these marital quagmires are the children involved. Should the children of divorced couples have to figure out how to weave through the train wreck of a broken marriage and our bad decisions? Many things in this world are simply unstoppable. And one of those things is that thing we call love. If there is but one lesson I have learned in this lifetime, I have learned that there is absolutely nothing you can do to make a person fall in love with you.

Likewise, you cannot do anything to prevent them from falling out of love, either. You can only be as cautious in entering a relationship as you would in entering a four-way intersection. What do you do when you reach a four-way stop? You approach the intersection slowly, come to a complete stop, review your surroundings, and proceed with caution when it appears safe to do so. Our approach to our relationships should be the same. Do you love yourself enough to protect yourself from all hurt, harm, or possible danger? I think the average person would answer that question in the affirmative. Nevertheless, did you know that opening yourself up to the possibility of love also means exposing yourself to pain? When it comes to love, there is no action you can take to guard yourself against the possibility of love loss.

Let's face it: people can make choices. Sometimes they will choose to love you, and other times they will choose to love someone else. So, yes, sometimes it can hurt and hurt badly. So, what choice do you have in this entire love conversation? Well, you choose to make sure that, when it's all said and done, you did your absolute best in making sure your decision to marry was based on fact—not fiction. A pastor once told me that you always want God to see you doing right.

In a society where people go in and out of relationships like fast food restaurants, it takes real maturity for a person to decide not to replicate the bad examples lived before them. Likewise, it takes a particular brand of courage to take the cautionary steps needed to ensure the best outcome for any people joined together in holy matrimony. Since my divorce, I have learned that marriage is much more than a label to solidify or affirm the boyfriend-girlfriend relationship. Marriage and the institution of marriage require mature adults.

Scientists in the medical profession believe that most men do not achieve true maturity until approximately 35 years of age, and it is widely believed that both men and women are most stable at this point in their lives. Whether you agree with this study or not, I think we all can agree that it takes mature people to handle mature situations and that marriage is a situation that requires extreme maturity. In the context of marriage, emotional maturity means that you have the grit to deal with the rollercoaster ride of marriage without running away or calling it quits at the first sign of trouble.

So, while you are investigating, exploring, or contemplating the idea of marriage, resolve that divorce is not an option. Suppose you determine that divorce is not an option beforehand. In that case, it will drive you to ask the questions that need to be asked and answered before the real possibility of marriage or saying, "I DO!" is even considered.

Mutual Accountability

In the age of political correctness, where people refrain from telling the truth about situations or circumstances to pursue that which is personal and almost always beneficial, it's very easy to associate with people who could easily be described as selfish or habitual liars.

The word "selfish" describes an individual who cares only about self, and to be precise, a habitual liar is a person who makes a habit of lying. It seems that selfishness and lying have become commonplace in our society. From the halls of justice to the religious sects of all denominations and religious affiliations worldwide, people have lost touch with the moral attributes of integrity and mutual accountability. I think you and I can agree that it must be built on a foundation of truth, not lies, for any relationship to work.

Likewise, relationships must be about the mutual needs of the many, not the one. Therefore, if these two characteristics are the basis for a relationship, a solid, longstanding, and loving marriage between a man and woman requires that both parties respect and honor one another. This attribute can easily be defined as mutual accountability. If you consider marriage, this must be an explicit attribute that you can identify in yourself and your potential spouse. What does it mean to be mutually accountable, and what attributes should we look for? Well, the Bible tells us the following:

Discernible Attributes

- Love each other. (John 15:17)

- Serve one another in love. (Galatians 5:13)

- Be kind and compassionate to one another. (Ephesians 4:32)

- Carry each other's burdens. (Galatians 6:2)

- Confess your sins to each other and pray for each other. (James 5:16)

- Be devoted to one another in brotherly love. Honor one another above yourselves. (Romans 12:10)

- Accept one another. (Romans 15:7)

- Encourage one another and build each other up. (1st Thessalonians 5:11)

- Spur one another on toward love and good deeds. (Hebrews 10:24)

Love and Don't Lie To Each Other

If you genuinely want to experience a marital relationship that is full of love and romance, then your relationship must be rooted in the characteristics of trust and honesty. If there is one thing that will cause your marriage to sink faster than the Titanic, it is having a relationship built on lies and deceit.

Therefore, we must be honest about absolutely everything—no matter the cost. The truth will sting a while, but a lie will sting forever. Relationships of all types can weather many storms, but the storm of deceit, more often than not, is a deal-breaker for most relationships. I remember being involved in a relationship with a woman who told one lie after another. Each lie killed and tore apart our relationship. Ultimately, the relationship itself ended. Throughout my life's journey, I have seen the claw of deceit rip through the foundations of rock-solid relationships more times than I care to remember.

If you want to take a sledgehammer to your happy home, you only need to begin operating from a place of deception. And that, my friend, is the cold hard truth. They engage in the art of deception to control the outcome and the lives of the people they are deceiving to prevent those people from making decisions based on truth and not fabrications. To that end, no one has that right. When I was a child, my mother told me that a person who will lie is a person who will steal. Likewise, a person who will steal is a person who will lie.

I was too young to understand the significance of what she was saying then, but now I know that my mother was trying to tell me that corruption of any kind leads to more corruption. If you are considering marriage, you should ensure that being truthful is not a problem for you or your spouse. Second, make sure that you consider marriage from a place of love, not lust. Once you have instilled in your heart a desire to be truthful and honest in a way that will be found pleasing in the sight of God, then and only then are you ready to open your heart and release yourself to the possibility of marriage. Equally important in this process is making sure that you and your future spouse are equally yoked and of the same mindset related to the characteristics of honesty and trust and the value this characteristic carries.

Serve One Another In Love and Kindness

Would you ever consider being in a relationship or, for that matter, marrying someone who was thoughtless or unkind? Unfortunately, many people say, "I DO!" to people who are indeed irresponsible, selfish, and uncaring. Getting involved with a thoughtless person is as dangerous as playing with a deadly snake; you will undoubtedly be bitten. In all seriousness, there are a lot of dead spouses—some whose remains have never been found, gone too soon simply because they allowed themselves to get emotionally attached and involved with people who cared more about themselves than the lives of others.

Typically, when we think of people who fit this cold-hearted model, we think of terrorists, rapists, mass murderers, and serial killers. However, do you realize that the person you may be considering marrying can be as cold-hearted and evil as any serial killer or rapist who ever walked this planet? Because of this reality, you need to do your due diligence in determining whether the person you are considering marriage to is really who and what they are presenting themselves as. Are they loving and kind or practicing deception to fulfill an ulterior motive?

Be Kind to One Another

I can assure you that there will be times in your marriage when tempers will flare, unkind words will be said, and feelings will be hurt. I certainly do not want to imply that every argument will lead to a crime scene investigation. However, I want to say that derogatory words and thoughtless acts can be very destructive to spouses emotionally and can be potential precursors to physical abuse. A woman meets a man who appears to be so sweet, charming, and thoughtful that he charms her right out of her panties. After a very brief relationship, he convinces her that he cannot live without her and asks her to marry him.

Without a pause or second thought, the woman says, "Yes, I will marry you." The two wed in a few short months, and a few weeks into the marriage, he is physically abusing her almost every day. In this particular example, the seed of thoughtlessness produced an abusive harvest. This tells us that thoughtlessness can manifest itself in various ways.

Carry Each Other's Burdens

A wife quit her job without telling her husband of her desire for a career change, let alone involving him in the decision. Her selfish, thoughtless action jeopardized the family's finances and immediate future. The wife decided without considering the totality of her choice and how it would affect her husband and children. Typically, people who are thoughtless and selfish make rash decisions without regard for anyone else. It takes discipline to build a good, solid relationship, and it takes equal discipline to work toward marriage. Both people must have a heart and a proper mindset for thoughtfulness and kindness to achieve this attainable goal.

Honor Your Marriage with Your Language

A man and his wife are having a knock-down, drag-out fight. In the heat of the argument, the man calls the woman he loves the 'B' Word. How do you come back from that? Calling your spouse harsh, inappropriate names simply because you have a different opinion is like having a deadly form of cancer. It will not kill you right away, but eventually, it will. Name-calling and hitting are inappropriate in any relationship.

Furthermore, neither extreme will win you the humanitarian of the year award. I have learned from my life's troubled relationship moments that apologies last a while, but harsh words and the memories of fists flying will last a lifetime. Friend, no matter how difficult or tricky the togetherness of marriage might be, being thoughtful means that two people respect each other on a human level. When people are genuinely kind, they pause to consider all variables and impacts before making decisions that will affect others. Having a mindset of thoughtfulness means that you follow that biblical standard that says, "Do unto others as you would have them to do unto you."

In other words, if you do not want your spouse to behave in a particular way with you, don't behave that way with them. Marriage is a partnership consisting of two people, not a sole proprietorship consisting of only one. Treat your relationship with the love of your life with love, admiration, and mutual respect, expecting nothing less than the same in return. Being thoughtful in your relationship regarding your spouse's needs and what they rightly deserve ensures that you will have done your part in establishing the foundation needed to build your marriage.

Accept One Another

It has been said that when two people meet each other for the first time, it is like the fireworks that light up the 4th of July skyline; it is an explosion of beauty and wonder. Most couples who have maintained these relationships for any time will tell you that these explosive feelings have increased throughout the years. Likewise, married couples will attest that a solid friendship is needed if a marriage is filled with happiness, fulfillment, and joy. Good friendships are built over time; they are not fleeting. Although marrying a person one dislikes seems farfetched, people do it every day.

Therefore, if you want a marriage that will last forever, make sure that the person you are considering marriage to is indeed your friend. Like most things in life, marriage has its highs and lows. The courting process gives two people the opportunity to determine whether they will be accepting of one another or not. The whole idea behind courting or dating determines whether a person is truly Mr. or Ms. Right. It would help if you used this time to decide whether or not you and the person you are considering marriage with are two wonderfully blended fireworks in the evening sky or two deadly sticks of dynamite waiting to explode.

Confess Your Sins to Each Other and Pray for One Another

As well as having the integrity to admit wrongdoing, mutual accountability also means being able to apologize for failures. No one ever wants to utter, "I was wrong," or, "I'm sorry." However, if you expect to have any success in marriage, you'd best make yourself familiar with these refrains. Let's face it: nobody is perfect, and in the closeness and intimacy of relationships, either you or your partner is bound to make mistakes. When they come up in relationships, the key to handling these sticky spots is squashing them very early.

The sooner you put a period after the disagreement, the sooner you can move on to the next phase of your relationship. An attorney once told me that 99% of his clients were individuals whose problems were self-inflicted or who were too stubborn to admit wrongdoing. He went on to say that it was because of this human frailty that he would put his kids through college, purchase a yacht, travel around the world, and retire before he reached the age of 50. How is that you ask?

According to him, people are incapable of admitting fault.Because of this, issues that could have been resolved between two parties often reach his desk. Due to this reality, he said, he would become a multimillionaire. More than two decades later, those unresolved squabbles he outlined to me helped him achieve all of his objectives. African American poet Nikki Giovanni remarked, "Mistakes are a fact of life. It is the response to the error that counts." Our inability to admit wrongdoing leaves us vulnerable to missteps and the consequences they may create. All of us are aware that life presents both ideal and less-than-ideal circumstances. Consequently, it is no secret that the difficulties we experience in life can sometimes lead us away from our divine purpose and lead us to pursuits that are laced with evil intentions.

At times, humankind appears to be ungrateful and unworthy of the many gifts that have been bestowed upon us by the Creator of the Universe. Disobedience is referred to in sacred texts as a cause of this phenomenon. In addition, this prescribed history would imply that humans are inclined towards indifference. This being the case, one of the points of indifference that is documented in the human experience revolves around the concept of pride. There are some things in our relationships that can be resolved with a simple "I'm sorry." Pride often prevents us from looking the person we have offended, in this case, a spouse, in the eye and confessing, "I made a mistake, and I apologize." There are other things, however, such as infidelity, for which an "I'm sorry" will not suffice.

It is suggested in the sacred text that God casts our transgressions into the sea of forgetfulness. However, this sentiment is not readily accepted or shared by spouses who are directly impacted by infidelity. Obviously, such an offense is difficult to forget in part because it is so traumatic. Having come to this bitter realization, we can now turn our attention to the other side of the offense equation—forgiveness. Without forgiveness, an apology is equivalent to knocking on a door and not receiving an answer. There is only one method of bringing closure to a bad chapter in a marriage, and that is forgiveness. Thus, if you are considering marriage, you should determine whether the person you are dating has a spirit of forgiveness and reconciliation.

Courage Through the Hard Times

A couple who shares a deep faith in the Creator and a deep understanding of one another will have a bond in courage that is unbreakable regardless of what life throws at them. We are able to endure life's circumstances when our core principles are based on moralistic standards. As it is with most problems, two people working to accomplish a solution is better than one. Consequently, having two forward thinkers bound by principles and courage is beneficial to any relationship.

Relationships are great when times are good, but will the person you're considering marrying stick with you when times are tough? What happens to your relationship if you lose your job, get sick, or hit a rough patch emotionally? Would the person you are considering spending the rest of your life with remain with you during times of stress and discomfort? Marriage, when viewed from this perspective, requires more than courage to say, "I DO!" It also requires soul searching, honesty, and the commitment to remain on solid ground even when things get tough.

Boldness To Win

The role of a man is very important in the family, and the role of a woman is equally important. The ability to battle through the rough times and the audacity and courage to keep God at the forefront of their marriage and family life are necessary for families to enjoy their good times. Everything begins with the two people considering walking down the aisle and starting a journey together. If you're thinking of getting married today, it would be wise of you to remember that even if everything around you is working against you. In these moments, both of you must offer support to each other.

CHAPTER 4 | **DEEP FACTS & TAKEAWAYS**

1. Most couples who undergo their first divorce are 30 years old.

2. Approximately 60 percent of all divorces involve individuals between the ages of 25 and 39.

3. On average, 66 percent of divorces are filed by wives. This number has risen to nearly 75 percent in recent years.

4. The following are the five professions with the highest divorce rates:

   - Dancers – 43%

   - Bartenders – 38.4%

   - Massage Therapists – 38.2%

   - Gaming Cage Workers – 34.6%

   - Gaming Service Workers – 31.3%

RELATIONSHIP IQ | **INSIGHTFUL QUESTIONS**

- What was your parent's marriage like?

- What characteristics of your parents' marriage would you like to see in yours?

- What characteristics of your parents' marriage would you like to avoid?

- How did your mother treat your father and vice versa?

- Would you like your marriage to follow the same pattern?

- Did you see your parents work through difficult periods in their marriage?

- Did you witness any physical, emotional, or sexual abuse in your household growing up or outside your household?

- Have you personally experienced any physical, emotional, or sexual abuse?

Chapter

5

PERILS OF

PREMARITAL SEX

The purpose of marriage as outlined in biblical scriptures differs from anything we see or experience today. People today appear to marry for all the wrong reasons. Among the many reasons people marry is to supplement income, and as a way to reduce the rising cost of living. Some will also engage in a fictitious marriage in order to benefit from the convenience of living with a sex partner. Whatever the reason, if the marriage is not defined by a genuine love for God, for oneself, and for the individual with whom one intends to spend the rest of one's life, it is destined to fail. The purpose of this book is to help you start your journey toward understanding what marriage is, what it does, and how to make your marriage work by providing you with the firm foundation you will need. An excellent marriage does not require a life of excess. All you need to know is what it takes to have one.

Principled Marriage

Marriage in fact is the union of two lives brought together by the bond of deep regard. It also offers a level of stability unmatched by any other human relationship. It fosters a sense of fulfillment for human relationship; it provides a sense of completion and fulfillment for those newlywed couple sold out to marriage and each other. In this sense, couples are assured of a more fulfilling relationship when they follow the wisdom of creation rather than the unwise ideals of humanity. Surely that is what the sacred scriptures represent, a plan for our development and well-being?

I am sure many simply see the Holy Bible, Qur'an, and Torah as ancient books from an age long gone with principles and philosophies no longer applicable in today's modern society. However, God's law supersedes any thought or opinion modern society has had, may have, or will have in the future.

Absolutely No Sex Before Marriage

People seem so eager to get their freak on that they ignore or forget the importance of getting their friendship on. Many divorced couples will tell you that they knew the person they married was not right for them. Because of this reality, sex before marriage is an absolute no-no. In this age of promiscuity, society has scripted out a context in which sexual immorality is acceptable and has been packaged and sold to millions of consumers as entertainment. Each year, literally thousands of sexually explicit songs, movies, television programs, books, artwork, and pictures are produced, dedicated to the sin-stained spirit of sexual immorality. Because of this reality, millions of people are influenced into violating God's moral code for humanity.

So, as you can see, it is not entirely your fault if you find it difficult to abstain from sex before marriage. In this modern society where everything goes, we are indoctrinated into an immoral lifestyle either directly or indirectly simply by the explicit themes that we see around us (i.e., magazines, music, porn, TV, etc.). However, God's laws and requirements for our lives have not changed and still stand today. The Bible indicates that God destroyed an entire city because of its immorality. A fact that is lost on many individuals who promote a lifestyle of sexual immorality (Genesis 18).

I cannot impress upon you enough the importance of not having sex before marriage. It is properly the best choice. But more significantly, it allows you to determine with a clear head and focus whether the person you are considering spending the rest of your life with is indeed the best person based on the facts and not the feelings associated with sexual contact.

In the film Boomerang, Eddie Murphy portrays the character "Marcus," an advertising executive who attracts and sexually exploits women without regard for their feelings. In the aftermath of a sexual encounter with his boss, he is treated in a similar manner. Having been completely turned on his head by this unexpected turn of events, Marcus' career and reputation as the office workplace Romeo suffer; so much so that Mr. Jackson, played by the late John Witherspoon, informs Marcus that his mixed fortune stems from his fascination with a woman's vagina and her insatiable sexual desires. He encourages Marcus to take control of the situation rather than letting it control him.

This scene highlights the fact that men and women have or will enter into a marriage relationship based on a desire for sex, or their addiction to having sex with a particular person. As one of the many dumb-dumbs to make this mistake, I live daily with the regret of the poor choice I made. On the day before my wedding, I intended to end the relationship totally and completely. However, after being convinced to spend one more night together, my lust overruled my maturity and all reasoning. This led me to make a dumb decision that I continue to pay for today. With regard to the mistakes I have made, I do not regret many of them. There is, however, one that I wish I could take back. And that is getting married without the guidance of premarital investigation and counseling and engaging in sexual relations before entering into a committed relationship.

Can it be difficult to refrain from having sex before marriage? Absolutely! But it is not impossible. Being a virgin and never having experienced sexual activity before marriage increases the chances of remaining celibate. In the event that you have opened Pandora's Box, you may have a lot of work to do in order to maintain sexual sobriety before marriage. Although it may seem difficult, maintaining celibacy can be achieved.

Avoid Temptation

If you wish to stay celibate, steer away from situations that cause you to lose focus and lead you into folly. There should be no intimate kissing, touching, rubbing, or long, intimate hugs with your potential spouse. You should also refrain from adult-related themes (i.e., pornography) that are sexual in nature and self-stimulation in the form of masturbation or erotic massage.

Develop A Support System

Let friends and family members know of your decision to remain sex-free before marriage. Find an accountability partner or group in your local church that can offer you leadership and support.

Tell Your Partner the Truth

Let them know that you are celibate and plan to remain that way until marriage if you are dating someone. If you are upfront, then they can decide whether they want to pursue or continue a relationship with you or not.

Engage in Dialogue with God

What does the word of God say about sex before marriage? Have you read the Holy Bible to see what your decisions mean for your life? Many religions and denominations promote celibacy and let you know why you should continue to abstain from sex. Speak to your pastor, elder, or another church leader about your decision and desire to remain sex-free until marriage.

Date Someone with the Same Belief System

Entering into a relationship with someone who has a like mind makes being in a relationship in most cases a lot easier. Suppose you are involved with someone who has a similar attitude about celibacy. In that case, you have a support structure within the relationship itself which means that you are less likely to engage in improper behavior than you are with someone who does not share the same belief system.

Prayer

Finally, make prayer a regular part of your strategy to remain celibate. In our intimate conversations with God, we find our strength in dealing with the struggles of our flesh and the urges of sexual desire.

The Importance of Abstinence

Abstinence can offer those who choose its sanctity the opportunity to live a life free of coercion and disease. It is estimated that more than thirty million people worldwide are infected with HIV/AIDS. After a physical before the 1991-92 NBA season, Ervin "Magic" Johnson discovered that he had tested positive for HIV. Johnson initially said he did not know how he contracted the disease but later acknowledged that it was through having multiple sexual partners during his playing career. It is only by the grace of God that Magic's wife, Cookie Johnson, whom he had recently married, did not contract the deadly virus.

In this very real situation, we see an all-too-clear reality of the dangers of having sex before marriage. There are times in life when careless decisions can lead us to hurt the ones, we most care about and love. However, there are times when our careless decisions can also double back to hurt ourselves. Sexual sobriety can save you from sexually transmitted diseases and may also safeguard your life from the sexually depraved and wicked.

Seeing Your Life Beyond Sex

Many people have gotten married only to find out that they never really knew the person they married. Spouses have ended up dead, missing, and on the backs of milk cartons with captions above their heads that read "Have You Seen Me?" simply because they tied themselves romantically to people, they never took the time to get to know. Regardless of what anyone says, sex always clouds the issue. Likewise, it prohibits us from making sound and wise decisions based on the evidence we can see.

Evaluating the Stakes

Friendships are based on four core factors: communication, respect, trust, and honesty. The stakes for your marriage's success are high, and it is risky to chance the possibility that any one of these core factors is not validated and verified before marriage. If your boyfriend is a jerk, why not find out before the expense of a costly wedding and honeymoon? If your girlfriend is a gold-digger, why not find out before a costly divorce and child support payments are imposed?

Time and Chastity

It is unfortunate that the pressures of career advancement, the burden of debt, raising children, and the rise of selfishness lead many couples to end their marriages before the ink has even dried on the marriage license. For this reason, it is imperative that couples who are considering marriage use time and virtue to create a solid foundation for their union. You should, above all, be the best of friends with your future spouse.

Time Has Advantages

A twenty-year-old man who weighs two hundred pounds has a far better chance of lifting forty pounds than a five-year-old. Why? Because the combination of time and maturity builds the strength, muscle, and endurance needed to shoulder the load. Shotgun weddings or those that come after lust-filled romps never last because, much like the five-year-old, they lack the time required to develop the maturity, strength, and endurance needed to go the distance. Shotgun marriages or quick nuptials fold at the first sign of crisis.

Boomerang Relationships

We would be remiss if we did not discuss those boomerang circumstances, better known as rebound relationships. Of all the relationships between men and women, this can be one of the most toxic and demoralizing. In this type of relationship, the person on the rebound attempts to continue their broken relationship with the new person with whom they are involved. In every relationship of this type I have been involved in with a person on the rebound, their bodies were always with me, but their minds were on the other side of town with those guys they were still pining for. Because of this desperate circumstance, I created within myself a reminder: never go grocery shopping on an empty stomach and never get married to someone on the rebound; if you do, you will always get more than what you bargained for.

Rebound Relationships

Rebound relationships are very tricky because you never know whether the person you are getting to know in truth and honesty is getting to know you for the same reasons. Again, in almost every instance, people rebounding from a previous relationship are continuing that relationship with the new person. The father of one of my friends married less than a year after his wife passed away and now is experiencing some regret, having realized that his marriage was a vain attempt to create a continuation of his former reality. New relationships should never be carryovers from previous ones. Ladies, you cannot make your current lover become what your last lover was. Gents, you cannot turn your golden lady of yesterday into what you have today.

Take Your Time and Do It Right

It would be wise to walk carefully through the minefield when considering a relationship with someone on the rebound. Depending on the depths of the person's former relationship and just how interested in this person you are, you may want to save your emotional connections or affections for someone else or at least for another time. If something about this person tells you they have the potential to be the one, then go for it. However, I would caution you to take your time, get to know the person very well, and refrain from sex, kissing, or anything that could produce sexual stimulation. I would focus on being a good friend, which means that you must focus on being a great listener.

The longer you wait and allow your potential dream man or dream girl to get over the previous relationship, the better. Remember, your healing can't be hurried.

Build Your Marriage Muscle

If the person you are considering is fresh out of a relationship, you may want to examine this person and get to know them during this period before even considering entering into a relationship with them, let alone marriage. The key to friendship is to be patient, consistent, and friends. A good friendship, full of love, trust, honesty, commitment, integrity, and faithfulness, is established over time. As the friendship grows and matures, it will develop the strength and grit needed to overcome the adversities often encountered by those in relationships. Therefore, friendships are not squandered or mired in controversy. They are esteemed and held to a higher standard.

When contemplating marriage, be sure you and your future spouse are truly friends. Should you feel uncertain or shaky regarding friendship, then hold your horses on the wedding carriage and continue to work towards establishing a friendship. In any situation, it is always easier to get into a jam than to get out of it. Having all the information prior to saying, "I DO!" will enable you to make the most informed decisions possible about your future, your life, and, ultimately, your happiness.

More Reasons

Many of the separations and divorces that occur in our world today result from the fact that not enough of the right questions are being asked before saying, "I DO!" As a result, marriage licenses are being shredded, and families are torn apart by divorce. If you are indeed considering marriage to the man or woman of your dreams, a good question to ask yourself is what your motive or motivation is for wanting to marry them. Is it for love, companionship, sex, money, laughter? What is your reason for wanting to be married? This is also a good question to pose to your potential significant other: Why do you want to marry me?

These questions are of great significance these days as more people are entering into the bonds of marriage with ulterior motives or reasons other than just the joys of marriage. These are circumstances in which one or both parties marry for a purpose other than love, typically marrying for gain or future advancement. Friend, people are prostituting themselves into marriage simply for the conveniences of being married. People are focused more on the opportunity of having someone to get sex from each night and share the cost-of-living expenses with rather than the joys of being in love.

It is quite easy to see why marriages of this variety do not last long. It is shocking when you stop to think that people had stood before God and LIED, knowing they had no intentions of carrying out the vows they promised to keep. Marriage is serious business, and because it is serious business, our decision to enter into this covenant relationship should not be taken lightly. It takes hard work, asking the right questions, proving things through examinations, praying to God, and waiting for his divine answer. It may seem corny, awkward, or even dumb at first to ask so many questions of a person with whom you are considering marriage. Nevertheless, the only dumb questions in life are the ones not asked.

You might want to consider the following questions before saying, "I DO!" to your potential partner:

- Why are we getting married? Pregnancy, financial security, loneliness?

- As a couple, what do we want out of life?

- What do you think our lives will be like in thirty or forty years?

- Do you drink alcohol? If so, how often do you drink?

- Have you ever physically assaulted anyone you were dating?

- Do you think it is important to be faithful to one another in a relationship?

- Do you have a criminal record, history, or background? If so, for what?

- How would you feel if I wanted a night out with my friends now and then?

- How will we make sure we have quality time together?

- How much time will we spend with our in-laws?

- Can we talk about money?

The Pregnancy Proposal

There are several reasons that people enter into marriage these days. However, I would bet my last dollar that the number-one reason people who are not ready for marriage venture into it is out of the obligation of pregnancy. If being in love is the single best reason for popping the question to your love, the single worst reason is that a baby is on the way. That is right! Pregnancy is the absolute worst reason to get married. Listen, you do not fix a mistake by making another mistake, and marrying someone, for this reason, is an absolute mistake. Obligating yourself to marriage because the stork is making a delivery in 9 months is the least intelligent reason for proposing marriage.

Let me be clear: marriage after conception does not change that a child was conceived out of wedlock. Subsequently, marriage will not absolve people of whatever guilty feelings they may have. Therefore, we should isolate those feelings of guilt and deal with them rather than compounding one problem with another.

The Financial Proposal

Much like the pregnancy proposal, if you marry someone for financial security, you make one huge mistake. I cannot say that I fault anyone for wanting to make sure they partner with someone financially secure. However, marriage for the sole purpose of financial gain is a loss. If there is one place where greed is most prevalent, it is among our financial elite in the worlds of sports and entertainment. Both men and women of status are simply looking for someone to love them, giving their hearts and ATM PIN code numbers to creeps only out for the cash. Certainly, we have all heard those stories where a gorgeous young woman marries a financially well-to-do man simply for financial gain.

Typically, everyone but the unsuspecting fool being bled dry can see that this type of woman is nothing more than the proverbial gold-digger. Subsequently, the man will lose the shirt off his back in this circumstance. Once the women decide the charade is over and implements that age-old legal maneuvering tactic called divorce and ask for half of everything without a flinch of the cheek. If you have been blessed with financial riches, carefully consider whom you marry and your marriage reasons, especially if you aim to remain financially sound. Another side of this circumstance needs to be highlighted, particularly for women who choose to marry a man of means simply for gain and not for love.

In this circumstance, women who marry men are often treated like property rather than people. Sometimes, they are mentally, verbally, and even physically abused because the man does not see them as equals or a partner. In fact, in most cases, the man sees you only as a reservoir for his seed or a toy for his sexual desire. He marries you for his purposes, for his gain, and discards you when he is finished with you. Ladies, you will never convince a man like this to love you. You will never change him or make him into a different person. It should also be said that marrying a woman solely for a source of financial stability is also an unwise decision for a man. Why do you ask? Well, for starters, the woman will never respect you. You were born to be the head, but you will most certainly be the tail in this type of relationship, as you have no say-so whatsoever.

If you marry a woman and move into her home, it is her home. In addition, when she decides that you are no longer the man of her dreams, you will be asked to leave her home. No woman or man should ever enter into a relationship, particularly a marriage, without being able to take care of him or herself fully--period. Regardless of what a person says or how much they assert that they love you or how many times they declare that what is theirs is yours, etc. If you trigger that person in a manner that rings their bell incorrectly, your limitations, whatever they might be, are bound to be brought up.

My income was in the six-figure range when I met the woman who would eventually become Ex-wife #2. Typical of most divorced and responsible non-custodial fathers, my primary earnings were garnished for child support while my second job was used to supplement the first. However, I was blessed in that both jobs paid pretty well. As soon as my then girlfriend and I decided to get married, she shared her concerns about my working two jobs. She said that my primary check and her regular check would be enough for us to live happily ever after. As a result of her encouragement, I quit my second job and made what would prove to be a very costly mistake. Being unable to do the things she had become accustomed to, I became a financial anvil around her neck.

A few short months after we married, our marriage came to an end, leaving me with a vehicle I could not afford, living accommodations that were unaffordable, a second full-time job, and high monthly bill obligations. If I had used a hint of wisdom and listened to that voice inside of me urging me to stop and think about what I was doing, the situation would have been different. You should never get married or enter into a relationship with anyone unless you have the financial means to do so. It is therefore important that you ensure you are financially independent before you consider marriage and that you are able to make decisions regarding your financial position on your own. Ensure you are in the best financial position to manage your affairs.

Curing Loneliness

If you consider marriage to solve a loneliness issue and, three days after marriage, your spouse has a fatal heart attack or runs off with another person, where does that leave you? It takes you right back to loneliness. Getting married to someone to cure the loneliness blues only leads to more loneliness. One of the major problems I noticed with ex-wife number two was her constant need to be the center of attention. She would spend hours looking at her face, her hind parts, and other parts of her body in the mirror and talking about the different surgeries she wanted to get to "improve herself." There was always a three-alarm crisis in her life that required immediate attention and a focus on her.

Speaking of attention, her primary goal was always to be the center of attention. If she wasn't the center of attention, it was a problem. Her inflated sense of self often caused conflicts with friends and family. By her own admission, she didn't have a good reputation. She seemed to be tolerated by people for their own interests. It was obvious to her that the men in her life wanted sex with her. However, if a sexual relationship was not in the cards, they were unwilling to continue to interact with her. A sexual liaison with a married man that resulted in the birth of her child did not eliminate her feelings of loneliness. The experience only contributed to an increase in isolation. Considering this moment in time, we should learn that we can never rectify mistakes by making bigger ones.

Entering into marriage simply because one is lonely is like accepting a loan contract that one cannot afford. Committing to a friendship, relationship, or marriage to cure loneliness is bad. You need to be "cool with yourself"! This means that you have a healthy love and respect for yourself regardless of who is or who is not around. This means that you bring to the table the relationship a person who is complete, whole, and happy with whom they are, with or without company. Relationships, especially marriages, should always be about what you can offer or bring to the relationship, not what you can get or take from it. If you fear loneliness, go to Church. Plenty of people in the Church suffer from similar issues and learn to deal with them. Could you not get married to solve them?

If you fear loneliness, find the underlying cause of your loneliness. I have found, in most cases, that lonely people are so because they do not have an inviting attitude. There are also occasions where people refuse to come out of their comfort zone. To make a friend, you have to be a friend. It all boils down to your motive and reasons for entering into relationships and friendships. If your heart was broken in a previous relationship, do whatever you have to do to learn from it, get over it, and live life forward.

Come and Talk to Me

It is a beautiful experience to be married when you can have enjoyable conversations. Healthy communication opens the door to all of marriage's warmest experiences, as most successful couples will attest. Having a relationship that allows you to express feelings, fears, concerns, and cares without fear of judgment or reproach can create a warm feeling and a pure zest for life that can only be achieved through oneness.

How Deep Is Your Love

Unfortunately, far too many marriages end up on the scrap heap of love because they never seem to be able to move past the topical experience, never daring to dig deep into the expanse of their partner's life, love, and inner spirit. Through my countless conversations with divorcees, I have surmised that many people in this census column never moved past the "like" stage, seemingly finding themselves or their relationship in that special place called love. Communication is integral to any healthy marriage, as being able to talk openly about any topic strengthens your relationship and affirms your commitment to each other. As the relationship progresses, direct, in-depth communication is not only good sense but also potentially lifesaving during the courtship stage.

Deep Dark Secrets

Let me ask you this: Do you know your potential partner's sexual history? How about their HIV/AIDS status? Based on the latest STD numbers and HIV/AIDS rate of infection statistics, if you are considering marriage to your potential significant other, it is a good idea for you both to know your status. Typically, couples like to avoid these conversations out of fear of turning their partner off. However, in today's society, you'd better ask the question. In America today, women find out in record numbers that their husbands entered into marriage with deep, dark secrets; women find out that their husbands are homosexuals. This lifestyle exposes an unsuspecting wife to the possibilities of a life-ending disease, not to mention the damage it causes to the bonds of marriage.

I do not know about you, but if I am considering marriage to someone, this is indeed something that I need to know about now and not after my hair starts falling out. I do not want a choice regarding my health and well-being, or, for that matter, the health of my offspring decided for me by someone who has been selfishly hiding a secret lifestyle.

Know Your Status

Unfortunately, the huge investigative oversight of failing to ask about HIV status has cost many women their lives, causing them to end up with AIDS or another dreaded disease. Many of us who slept around before marriage made the huge error of entering into sexual relationships without regard for the physical consequences. We ripped our underwear off without an ounce of knowledge regarding our partners sexual history. Only time will tell whether we were fortunate enough to escape our bad decisions unscathed. However, others were not as fortunate; their loved ones were forced to watch them waste away because information regarding sexual behaviors was never addressed.

Again, we should move beyond the purely topical to a place where real communication can provide us with the truths, we need in order to make sound decisions. Regarding sex, I would like to discuss another angle. No, this conversation is not about sexual positions but rather about sex and the importance of abstinence from sexual activity while weighing marriage considerations. If you genuinely want to make an informed decision to wed or not, it would be best if this decision is made without the influence of sex.

Sex was never intended to be casual, or something high school seniors look forward to on prom night. Other than diseases, did you know that having sex before marriage introduces many messy behaviors into relationships? When you are engaged in sexual activity before marriage, you are reducing your ability to use wise judgment and wisdom, qualities essential for a successful relationship. A clean mind can make clear, precise decisions inspired by reason rather than sexual or carnal desires. Your marriage decision should be based on tangible things—not sexual. An effective way to measure this is by what I like to call the "deaf, mute, maimed" scenario. If you want to determine whether you are really in love with and have a true love for your potential significant other, you need to ask yourself the following questions:

- How would I react if my girlfriend/boyfriend were involved in a horrible accident that left them deaf, unable to speak, and totally paralyzed?

- If my girlfriend/boyfriend were to be stricken with an illness preventing sexual activity, what would I do? Could I remain in a committed relationship even if my sexual desires were not satisfied?

- Do I intend to remain with my girlfriend/boyfriend to whom I am considering marriage until death separates us?

While these examples may appear over the top, they are realities faced by couples every day. Now, you need to decide whether you can cope with this reality. You can clearly consider this question without bias when your sexual desires are not competing with your brains' ability to arrive at logical conclusions.

Orgasmic Complications

Sex or orgasm complicates your ability to make the necessary judgments needed to determine whether you have what I like to call staying power or, quite simply, the ability to meet all the terms of the marriage contract without defaulting.

Pornography Goes Mainstream

You cannot turn on a television or radio broadcast these days without being inundated with images and sounds related to sex. You cannot pick up a magazine without seeing breast-o-plenty, tight waists, nice hips, firm shapes, six-pack abdominal muscles, and other images of lust. Even pornography, once considered a filthy, perverse genre of adult cinema, has now made its way from the dark corridors and seedy streets of the slums into America's mainstream.

The World Is Rated X

Even our politicians, religious leaders, and public officials held to a certain moral standard are not immune, ultimately leading to public scandal, apologies saturated in spin, and, unfortunately, broken marriages and families. The sin drivers of Madison Avenue will tell you that sex sells. Consequently, our lives are surrounded by images that woo us into banging or screwing whoever we want whenever we want without any thought of repercussions. Since this is the major consensus of society and certainly accepted by mainstream America, it is important to unplug our minds from the matrix of madness that promotes an attitude of immorality or, at the very least, an ideology very resistant to the Creator's plan for our lives and male-female relationships.

When it comes to matters of importance, the subject of sex should be the farthest thing from your mind during the courtship process. I cannot stress this point enough in this X-rated world: sex before marriage pollutes your judgment and affects your ability to make the best choices. Maintaining a sex-free relationship during the courtship process may prove difficult. Therefore, you will need to employ some strategies that will aid you in this most important effort:

- Have dinner in open settings with close friends and family members.

- Engage in absolutely no intimate contact, tongue kissing, or intimate touching.

- Refrain from having conversations about sexual intercourse.

- Stay away from adult-themed movies or music saturated with sexual overtones.

If your relationship with your potential significant other is important to you, it behooves you to use every technique available to help you make this most crucial decision. If accomplishing this goal means that you have to employ the services of a good confidant, then, by all means, do so. Regardless of what society thinks or says, there is no harm and no shame in wanting to do things the right way. Let us say the individual you are considering for marriage is not the right match. In this case, you may be able to part ways amicably without the lingering effects of sexual addiction impairing your decision-making process.

CHAPTER 5 | **DEEP FACTS & TAKEAWAYS**

1. It is estimated that 48 percent of those who marry before the age of 18 are likely to divorce within 10 years compared with 25 percent of those who marry after the age of 25.

2. Sixty percent of couples who marry between the age of 20 and 25 are likely to divorce.

3. Those who delay marriage until they reach the age of 25 are 24 percent less likely to divorce than those who marry earlier.

RELATIONSHIP IQ | **INSIGHTFUL QUESTIONS**

- Were you aware of any infidelity by either of your parents or other family members?
- If yes, how did the spouse who was cheated on react and deal with this situation?
- What effect did the infidelity have on you and other family members?
- Did your family spoil you? Did you usually get what you wanted?
- Did your parents avoid any type of disagreements or confrontations?
- Did your parents spend most of their leisure time together, or apart?

- Were you aware of one parent hiding items or keeping secrets from the other?
- In your family, who was the main decision maker?

Brethren, even if anyone is caught in any trespass, you who are spiritual, restore such a one in a spirit of gentleness; each one looking to yourself, so that you too will not be tempted.

Galatians 6:1

Chapter

6

OVERCOMING
ADVERSITY IN
YOUR MARRIAGE

Contrary to what is often depicted in Hollywood films, married couples often and regularly face trials and tribulations. "Adversity" is defined by Webster's dictionary as "a state, condition, or instance of serious or continuing difficulty or adverse fortune." Humans are subject to a great deal of adverse fortune in their daily lives, much of which is self-inflicted. Humankind's indifference brought about a new age not intended by creation. The rebellion of humanity has caused a tidal wave of sorrow and suffering for all generations in history. The rebellious nature and behavior of some of us can be crippling, demoralizing, and destructive. In many respects, the earth is in turmoil due to humankind's emergence into this world, and it is continually on the brink of disaster with each breath that we as individuals take.

Weapons of Mass Destruction

Essentially, the world is in flames, both literally and metaphorically. It is the human race that is responsible for the fire. The right to control one's body is largely denied to women. There are many ways in which men have failed to be leaders in their homes, their communities, and in general, wherever true leadership is needed. In recent years, the family has suffered a severe decline. Today, sex is seen more as a recreational activity than a means of reproduction. Increasingly, our children are becoming unruly and out of control. The streets are literally drenched in their blood. Earth is on fire, there is no doubt about it.

Our day-to-day reality manifests humanity's rebellious nature. We may be doomed by said rebellion at some point. Human frailty and necessity are weapons used by those who regard themselves as superior. As a result, there are segments of our population who use our conditions, ideologies, creeds, colors, religious beliefs, and practices as weapons of mass destruction. This is done to create discord and disharmony for monetary gain, power, and influence. In light of this, there are a number of contemporary devices that may affect or disrupt your marital union.

Weaponized Human Weaknesses and Necessities:

- Appearance
- Approval Addictions
- Bankruptcy
- Bills
- Car Repossession
- Child Support
- Classism
- Credit Card Debt
- Egotism
- Employment Loss
- Foreclosure
- Illness
- IRS Wage Garnishment
- Lack of Education
- Low Self-Esteem
- Materialism
- Narcissistic Personality Disorder
- Obesity
- Predatory Lending
- Pride
- Racism
- Sexual Abuse
- Tax Property Liens
- Terminal Illness
- Theft of Savings
- Zero Retirement Plan

If you are considering marriage, you should be well-prepared for the adversities and distractions of life. More importantly, you need to guard your relationship as best as you can against these possible intrusions. The development of your relationship pre-marriage and post-marriage prepares you for the adversities of life that are sure to come. Remember, marriage is all about teamwork. It is about a husband and wife vowing to take on whatever the world brings them—together.

Adultery

Did you know that over 50% of the divorces in this country result from adultery? If you are indeed considering marriage, it would be wise of you to ask yourself whether you can marry this person and remain faithful. This may be one of the hardest questions a man will ask himself during the courtship and marriage process because men are hunters. I am not implying by that statement that women are prey that men hunt for sport. No, I am speaking to our pursuit of the feminine sex. Studies show that, on average, men think about sex every 7 seconds. If these studies are true, this means that, in the short time that it has taken me to write this paragraph, I have spent a considerable amount of time thinking about sex.

When men reach that magical time of puberty and the hormones begin to get in gear, their curiosity develops; their desire for female companionship grows stronger. He is driven like a fire to seek out or hunt for someone to be his mate. It may take several years for him to find the one woman who meets his needs.

But when he finds her, the intuitive nature or drive that he used to find her does not automatically turn off. The intuitive nature, drive, energy, or whatever you want to call it never turns off. Subsequently, the energy released within the male body that drives him to pursue a woman like there is no tomorrow must be redirected to another place. If not, this energy will go unchecked and be redirected to another woman, ultimately causing the sin of adultery to occur. Typically, when men cheat on their wives, they often try to find some reason to justify their indiscretions.

In some cases, men have given the following reasons for being unfaithful:

- The wife is no longer sexually attractive.
- Despite his best efforts, his wife is a constant complainer.
- It will be easy for him to get away with it.
- He has both space and opportunity.
- Infrequent sex with his wife (not enough sex).
- The ratio of women is higher than men making more sex available.
- His married life has become boring.
- He is no longer in love with his spouse.
- It is a boost to the male ego.
- It is an exciting challenge.

Since women are wired differently from men, their entrance into the world of cheating starts from a whole different place, yet there is a great deal of similarity with their male counterparts:

- She believes her husband is no longer sexually attractive.

- Her husband is a constant complainer.

- She can easily get away with it.

- She has space and opportunity.

- Sexual infrequency (not enough sex with her husband).

- Married life has become boring.

- She is no longer in love with her spouse.

- It is a boost to the female ego.

- It is an exciting challenge.

Regardless of the justifications or reasons both men and women use in committing infidelity, biblical scriptures make it pretty clear: adultery is a bad deal and hurts everyone caught in its grasp. There are two types of adultery. First, there is the infidelity of the flesh. This is when a committed married person enters into a sexual relationship with someone other than their spouse.

Typically, this brand of cheating lands you in divorce court or, if you step out on the wrong person, you may end up in the hospital or worse. You would think that this form of unfaithfulness is the most common. However, the most widespread form of cheating is when someone looks at another and undresses them with their eyes.

"You have heard that it was said, 'Do not commit adultery.' But I tell you that anyone who looks at a woman to lust after her has already committed adultery with her in his heart. If your right eye causes you to sin, gouge it out and throw it away. It is better for you to lose one part of your body than for your whole body to be thrown into hell...."

- Matthew 5:27-29

The scriptures tell us the story of King David and how he impregnated a woman named Bathsheba, the wife of one of his soldiers, and had this soldier sent to the front lines and killed to cover up the adulterous act.

As a result, we come to the point where we should discuss a different aspect of adultery that most people overlook, namely integrity. A person who enters into an adulterous affair while married cannot be trusted. Based on this fact, if you suspect your significant potential is cheating or if they have admitted they have cheated, this is a warning sign that you may want to stop, pump the brakes, do a double-take, and consider everything that is going on. Again, I am a proponent of the notion that how you start is how you finish. If your relationship starts based on lust, you will have an iniquity-filled relationship, one riddled with the bullets of deceit and ultimate despair.

Marriage is probably the most serious decision one will make in a lifetime. Again, I can tell you from my own experience that entering into marriage is not a decision one should make without wise counsel. If you are considering marriage and you have a cheater's heart, you may want to think seriously about deciding to enter into marriage. Have you stopped to consider the deadly ramifications associated with adultery? In years past, if a man caught his wife in the act of adultery and murdered her and her lover, he walked without doing any time. This type of murder was referred to as a crime of passion. This is where the impulse of jealousy, heartbreak, or rage causes a temporary break with reality, leading to the crime of murder.

Even something as seemingly minor as failing to put your belongings in the closet or leaving a spoon in the sink may set off an alarm for another individual's system of values, which brings us to the trickiest part of the shared value discipline. There is a common misconception that tolerance and acceptance are the same things. However, they are not synonymous. Despite the costs, it is imperative that individuals maintain the standards of their value system. Essentially, if you meet someone who has the qualities you are searching for in a spouse. But some of their qualities violate your value system; applying tolerance to those annoyances will not provide you with the solace or the sustaining power needed for your relationship to endure.

Applying tolerance to your annoyance will only make you more annoyed over time, particularly when life's everyday rigors or annoyances are at work. Therefore, it is best to identify during your courting stage if you are indeed equally yoked or, in secular terms, of the same value system. If you find that you do not agree, do not settle with the idea that tolerance can allow you to make your way through it. No one settles with the idea of having a rotten tooth in their head, opting to tolerate the pain by popping an Advil and the smell by chewing a piece of mint.

The correct course of action would be to remove the tooth or, in this case, the annoyance. If you would not settle for having a tooth decaying in your mouth, why would you settle for a relationship of the same status? God can get the best out of married couples who are equally yoked. When two people share the same value system, they share a belief that most teams share: they have what it takes to get the job done.

Typically, equally yoked people share the same beliefs in God, and their spiritual walk is synchronized. Likewise, those tied together by love and license are comfortable in their skin. In other words, they are not still in search of whom they are or what they are. These people already know who they are and their purpose in life. Moreover, these are people who are mature, stable collaborators and are ready to engage in the serious business of being in a committed relationship. These couples are truly in lockstep on every mile in this life journey. Is there disagreement at times? Sure, there is! However, the disagreement is never enough to override the directives coded into the shared system of values. Therefore, a misunderstanding is similar to a fly on the windshield in that it is only a momentary blur. In the same way one would not dispose of a $40,000 vehicle because of a bit of bug splatter, why would one discard a healthy marriage because of a misunderstanding?

People with the same system of values share the same streams of thought. In other words, there is a commonality among those of like mind. Equally yoked couples can change the world. If we were to take a look at the most powerful philanthropists of our time, we would see that their ability to give in abundance flows from a circle of shared love, where the values of a couple in love allow them to be a blessing for those who are destitute and in need. A relationship between two selfless or equally yoked people works to serve humanity; however, a relationship between two people unequally yoked works toward humanity's destruction.

Unfortunately, I am guilty of this latter transgression. Due to my lust for a woman, I once sacrificed my value system by marrying her regardless of the fact that I was unequally matched with her. In this moment of my life, I turned my back on wisdom and wise counsel. I put my value system aside in order to end my drought of loneliness. I don't mean this disparagingly, nor am I trying to jeer either of my ex-wives, but a lonely man will marry a prostitute if he can convince himself that she loves him. There is no exception to this rule. As a result of this sad reality, many people abandon what they know is right for things they know are wrong.

Friend, no one wants to be alone. However, we should never compromise our faith in God or our value system simply to shed a period of singleness. I have learned that life is to be enjoyed when in love with someone or just loving oneself. Regardless of one's relationship status, keep your value system in balance with what you know in your heart is right. Your marriage to anyone at any time will only be as successful as the applied values.

Remember, acceptance, not tolerance, should be applied to the person you are considering marriage to. If you find yourself constantly in a posture of tolerating your mate and not being accepting of them, end the relationship now and start anew because this person, in all likelihood, is not one of your dreams but, rather, one of your horror-filled nightmares.

Many people have asked themselves days after getting married, "What the hell have I gotten myself into?" My reply is, "Hell is what you've gotten yourself into!" It is for this reason alone that it is critical that you do not compromise your values throughout the entire courtship process. Passion for your spouse is another crucial component of avoiding the pitfalls of adultery. If you want to have a winning marriage, you have to have a passion for every aspect of marriage and, for that matter, who you are marrying. The most successful people in life are so because of their focus, dedication, and passion for and toward the things they want most out of life. All of the greatest athletes are hailed as champions because their passion for their respective sport led them to the winner's circle time and time again. If you want to be in the winner's circle with your marriage, you can be.

Being in the winner's circle starts with making sure you have selected the right person to share your life with. Most people marry unsure whether they are making the right decision or not, opting simply to hope for the best.

Unfortunately, the commitment of entering into marriage requires more than a lukewarm or tepid approach. Friend, I cannot drive the point home enough that how you start is how you finish. If you take a lukewarm walk down the aisle with an unsure mindset toward the person you are marrying, you are surely destined for marital Armageddon.

I have interviewed several divorced people who have said that, on their wedding day, they were either unsure about what they were doing and sometimes even less sure about the person they were marrying. Why is that you ask? Well, it is because one or both marriage partners lacked the passion and commitment needed to make the marriage commitment work.

Having a committed and passionate relationship breeds an attitude that says to your partner, "It's you and me against the world." This kind of mentality is very difficult to overcome. When you and your spouse share a passion for each other, you do not wait for opportunities to present themselves. You allow your passion to create those opportunities. Those who are passionate, committed, and purpose-driven are unstoppable.

This is beneficial when two individuals are serious about their relationship and adamant about making it work. Assume that you are indeed considering marriage. In that case, you must have a winning attitude by expressing passion for your spouse, marriage, and personal goals. When you see your spouse, you should feel an uncontrollable level of excitement. Marriage offers so many wonderful things you can commit yourself to and accomplish that you should burst with pride. I strongly believe that gratitude is the best way to express your appreciation for your partner every day.

For two people who genuinely love each other and are committed to making their relationship work, this is of great value. Let's assume that you are indeed considering a marriage commitment. A successful marriage requires a winner's attitude, which involves a passion for your spouse, your marriage, and a sense of determination to succeed. Whenever you see your spouse, you should feel a sense of uncontrollable excitement. You should burst with joy when you consider all the wonderful things you can achieve and commit yourself to through your marriage.

Unfortunately, the everyday demands of life prevent people from remembering the days when love was elusive. Once again, you should thank your partner every day for being everything you ever wanted and more than you ever expected. Additionally, you will have to do everything in your power to ensure the long-term sustainability of your relationship. When couples earn each other's love, they must also maintain it.

With that said, it is time to ask a question. Would you have trouble imagining life without your person of interest, or are you unsure of your true feelings about them? If you find yourself struggling to answer this question, allow me to help. If there is any uncertainty in your mind, do not proceed with marriage or even a serious relationship until those doubts are addressed. If, however, you feel a passionate connection with the person you desire, and that connection comes from a pure place, then go for it. Keep in mind, however, that you need to be cautious.

The Principle of Trust

When adultery breaks the bonds of fidelity, one of the first things to leave the committed relationship is trust. Have you ever been punched so hard that it knocked all the wind out of your body? Any spouse who finds out their husband or wife has been having an affair will tell you that this is what it feels like. Again, many of the hardships we face within the human experience are self-inflicted. We have a choice about who we get into these relationships with. Based on this infallible truth, each of us needs to do a better job on the front end of protecting our emotions. Let me tell you something: relationships of all kinds are established or based on two fundamental principles—truth and trust. They are indeed the cornerstones to any successful relationships—period. You cannot have trust without truth.

To say that one has trust without first establishing truth indicates a great reason to distrust. When one establishes truth, he has gathered or grouped a series of real, solid facts that have been proven. When one proves a fact, he puts the facts to the test or through a series of trials to see whether the facts are indeed true and correct. This methodology or process of proving something is used every day in our courthouses, airports, business, or establishments where the need to establish a "now truth" is required. A "now truth" is when establishing a truth is needed quickly. Typically, this type of truth is needed before accessing a particular area or setting. A series of focused examinations must be conducted to establish trust.

In the examples provided, one must establish that no banned items or substances are detected items that could cause physical harm. Once truth has been established, trust is created, allowing the relationship between both parties to continue or begin. Relationships of all kinds should be based on a similar methodology. Many of today's marital relationships end because this fundamental methodology was missed. Many of us are guilty of rushing into relationships without first proving that what we see with our eyes is a true representation of what is there.

Unfortunately, many people who find themselves in situations of divorce today do so because they put their trust in people who did not deserve it and built foundations of false love on sinking sand. I am not ashamed to admit that I was one of those people. When I pledged my love in marriage in February 2007, I did so with a sincere heart. But truthfully, no matter how sincere your heart is, if you have not done your homework to prove the person, you are pledging your love to mirrors the same sincerity, you have done a poor job of securing your emotional borders. Subsequently, you have opened yourself up to the tortures of the pulling of your emotional heartstrings. With all that said, have you established a relationship with the person you are considering marriage to? Have you examined them, studied their character, and made the valuable assessments needed to determine whether they are for real or a simple fraud?

Also, have you made these valuable assessments without bias? It is rather difficult to make a true assessment of one's character if the flesh is biased. Again, this is another example of why sex before marriage never works because it prohibits you from making a true assessment based on substance and not sexuality. If I had known what I know now about relationships, truth, trust, and the importance of making accurate character assessments free of the bias of sex, my life today would be vastly different. I find it most interesting that we give the keys to our hearts and bodies to people who have a poor history, but we hide the keys to our hearts from God, who has an impeccable history of being heart-helping, not heart-hurting. Establishing a relationship with God is the first and most crucial step in having a successful relationship with any human being, let alone a marriage. Knowing where your relationship with God stands should be your first consideration if you are considering marriage today. If you are considering marriage, trust will play a big part in your marriage's success. However, I would submit that the trust you should put the most value into is your trust in God.

This wisdom is true not only for you but also for your potential significant other. God admonishes us to place our trust in Him, not mankind. Proverbs 3:5-6 reads, "Trust in the LORD with all thine heart; and lean not unto thine own understanding. In all thy ways acknowledge him, and he shall direct thy paths.

The late President Ronald Reagan's use of the phrase "trust but verify" tells us that it is not enough to simply trust— that trust must be based on empirical evidence, evidence that can be verified. In our society today, all kinds of checks and balances are used to verify or validate something before offering a stamp of approval. But what about our relationships, where is the verification process for that? Our verification process for our relationships can be found in the context of God's word. Moreover, his approval or denial of something can be heard if you are tuned into His frequency, exercising one's ability to hear His voice and move in His direction. Our ability to trust our spouse in a relationship starts with having a mind toward God and a heart for doing and trusting in what He says, not man. This means that we move from what we know in the natural world to what we know in the spiritual world.

"...and be not conformed to this world: but be ye transformed by the renewing of your mind, that ye may prove what is that good, and acceptable, and perfect, will of God."

Romans 12:2

We must first renew our minds about what the Creator says about truth, trust, and everything in this world. To nurture and cultivate these unique relationships, we must dedicate ourselves to Him and seek His guidance daily through studying His word and meditation. The two of you must work hard together in order to create a winning marriage. To achieve this, you should add the following disciplines to your daily routine:

- Taking the time to seek the Creator and being diligent about it takes daily effort on your part.

- Keeping your attention on the Creator daily is fundamental, as is diligence in your effort.

- Maintaining a healthy spiritual discipline.

- You are committed to keeping the Creator at the head of your relationship.

It is imperative to remember that relationships are built on two fundamental principles: truth and trust. The combination of fact and faith creates a bond unmatched by any other bonding agent between marriage partners and the Creator. Upon calling something into existence, the Creator shapes, and molds it so that it will serve specific purposes. Apple trees do not produce oranges because the Creator did not design them for this purpose. The Creator created the apple tree to make apples, which is its only purpose. Similarly, he established humanity for a specific and unique purpose.

CHAPTER 6 | **DEEP FACTS & TAKEAWAYS**

1. When an individual earns over $50,000 per year, the risk of divorce can be reduced by as much as 30% compared to those with annual incomes under $25,000.

2. The likelihood of divorce increases by 45 percent for men and women if they feel that their spouse spent money foolishly.

3. At least 30 percent of couples who argue about finances at least once a week will divorce.

4. According to the same study, couples without assets at the beginning of a three-year period are 70 percent more likely to divorce by the end of the period than couples with assets worth $10,000.

RELATIONSHIP IQ | **INSIGHTFUL QUESTIONS**

- Would you describe your parents as living in traditional male/female roles?

- Do you aspire to hold traditional male/female roles in your household?

- How would you describe your relationship with your mother?

- How would you describe your relationship with your father?

- How would you describe your relationship with your siblings?

- How are you most like your father?

- How are you most like your mother?

- Is it important to you that your parents approve of our relationship?

- If your parents don't approve of our relationship, how will it affect our marriage?

- If your parents and I have a disagreement, whose side will you most likely take?

- Whom would you rather disappoint, your parents or me?

Wherefore they are no more twain, but one flesh. What therefore God hath joined together, let not man put asunder.

Matthew 19:6

Chapter

7

Making Your Marriage Unbreakable

Now that we've discussed some concepts that will put both you and your potential spouse in the best possible position for marriage, it's time for us to discuss a topic that's an absolute must before saying I do, and that subject is premarital counseling. If you're considering marriage, it's time to start talking premarital counseling. So, what is premarital counseling, and why do you need it? Premarital counseling is a type of analysis that helps couples prepare for marriage. Premarital counseling can help ensure that you and your partner have a solid, healthy relationship giving you a better chance for a stable and substantial marriage.

Premarital counseling can also help you identify weaknesses that could become greater difficulties during the marriage. Typically, when premarital counseling is brought up, one person in the relationship may resist, expressing that the need for premarital counseling is ridiculous. They will say, "I don't need someone who doesn't know anything about us or our relationship telling us how to feel or act towards each other." Unfortunately, this sentiment causes many people to miss the unique opportunity premarital counseling offers.

Contrary to what some potential spouses might believe, premarital counseling is not an indictment against a couple's relationship. If fact, it's just the opposite. A couple's decision to obtain premarital counseling is an early proof of their desire, love, and commitment towards each other to make sure the decision to marry is based on facts and not mere feelings (i.e., great sex, feel good, etc.). Premarital counseling is a necessary course of action. It tips the scales of wisdom to your relationship's favor, helping both you and your potential significant other determine whether marriage to each other is truly meant to be. Any businessperson worth their salt will tell you that they don't make a critical business decision without first consulting wise counsel. In the book *Think and Grow Rich*, Napoleon Hill established the value of having smart people or access to wise counsel at one's disposal.

In fact, before his death, Hill suggested that many of the twentieth-century innovators, whom, I might add, we benefit richly from today, were innovators in their rights simply because they shared this valued belief. There is something to be said for sound advice. However, in these days and times, it is often difficult to discern who to trust as more and more, people of great intellect are out to serve their interests. It's safe to say that the economic downfall experienced in this country today is, in part, the result of greed and self-serving interest. Well, you're probably asking, how does all of this relate to premarital counseling?

Well, that's a good question. If you are considering getting married, you should know that there are a variety of premarital counselors and consultants who are ever so anxious to see you married but have not an ounce of concern for you, your potential spouse, or that matter, the longevity of your marriage. These evil characters are very similar to the politicians in Washington and the bankers on Wall Street who have bankrupted this country in that they only care about themselves. Therefore, you must make sure that the premarital counselors you're seeking for advice are credentialed counselors or therapists. It would help if you located therapists or counselors with a graduate or postgraduate degree. Moreover, search for a counselor credentialed by the American Association for Marriage and Family Therapy (AAMFT).

When you begin your search for a premarital counselor, you should take steps to be sure that you select someone who can support you. And remember, the counselor who can help your marriage helps you and your potential significant other. Make sure your spouse is an active participant in this selection process. The first step in locating a premarital counselor starts with calling one therapist office at a time and asking the following questions:

- How many years have you been a counselor?
- What are your credentials (e.g., academic degree)?
- Do you help your clients avoid some of the emotional hazards of marital adjustment?
- Do you help motivate your clients to complete the program successfully?
- Do you suggest strategies to solve your clients' marital problems?

These are only a handful of questions you can ask during your search for a counselor, but I think you see the importance of making sure you're hiring a counselor that will be of value to you and your relationship and not merely for their pockets.

On Earth As It Is In Heaven

If you are seeking wise counsel, you should begin by looking at the source of all-wise advice. From everlasting to everlasting, God has provided wise counsel and wisdom. Who better to ask about our lives than the Creator? For example, let's say that you owned a Cadillac Escalade that required warranty-related repairs. Would you take your SUV to the nearest Lincoln dealership for maintenance or return it to the appropriate manufacturer? This analogy applies to you and me in terms of the circumstances and issues that impact our lives.

In my opinion, God makes the best consultant. In every decision, God wants to be involved, whether it is about the person you are considering marrying or something as simple as purchasing a ring. Perhaps you are wondering, "I want to include God in my decision-making process, but how can I tell if what I am hearing is God's voice? To begin with, I would say that discerning the voice of God is extremely difficult if you don't know what you are listening for. As a result of the great wickedness and ugliness in our world today, it can be difficult to discern God's voice. But not impossible.

The times we live in today can be challenging. As such, wickedness is very easy to hear. To do so, you only need to tune into your personal device, walk out your front door, or turn on the radio in your vehicle. But the absolute failure in our inability to hear God's voice has more to do with our ears not being trained to His frequency. Are you aware, or perhaps better stated, do you understand, that every single day, God transmits a message to us that says:

- "I'm here for you!"
- "I want the best for you!"
- "I'll never leave you!"
- "I'll never forsake you!"

Unfortunately, we are so preoccupied with the daily rigors of life; that we are unable to tune in to God's voice and, in most cases, be aware of His presence.

Marriage is a big deal! As someone who has experienced both marriage and divorce, I understand the importance of following the matrimony process most appropriately. Thus, I would recommend that you consult with God for His divine wisdom and counsel if you're sincere about getting married. Marrying without pursuing the Creator's divine counsel is a huge mistake. Having established the importance of consulting God first, the next thing we must address is hearing the voice of God. How does one hear the voice of God?

Well, there are four sure-fire ways to hear God's voice in your spirit clearly and distinctly and know that it's Him. Now because we live in a corrupt world, this will not be easy—by any means. Getting a message from God will require effort, perseverance, commitment, and an undeterred desire. If you expect a booming voice to call your name in the middle of the night, I would not count on that happening. There is, however, a very subtle voice that whispers instructions to each of us, offering guidance and wisdom, and if we learn to recognize this voice, we will be ever so close to hearing our Creator with ease.

4 Basic Methods to Hear THE VOICE OF God

PRAYING

PRAYER IS THE ACT OF COMMUNICATING WITH GOD REVERENTLY

CONFESSION

RECOGNITION OR DISCLOSURE OF SIN OR SINFUL BEHAVIOR

DEVOTION

AMONG DEVOTIONAL ACTIVITIES ARE PRAYERS, READING SACRED SCRIPTURES, JOURNALING, MEDITATION, AND WORSHIP

COUNSEL

COUNSELING BASED ON BIBLICAL VALUES AND PRINCIPLES

It should be stated that these are not the only ways to hear God's voice. However, these methods are the most common regardless of one's level of faith or Christian maturity. Beginning with the first method, prayer, let us examine each technique closely to get our spirit tuned to God's frequency, allowing us to hear His voice.

Prayer

1. The road to hearing God's voice and knowing His will for your life begins with prayer. Here's what the scripture says regarding prayer:

   A. "This is the confidence we have in approaching God: that if we ask anything according to his will, he hears us. And if we know that He hears us—whatever we ask—we know that we have what we asked of Him" (1 John 5:14-15).

B. "Be joyful always; pray continually; give thanks in all circumstances, for this is God's will for you in Christ Jesus" (1 Thessalonians 5:16-18).

C. ". . . The prayer of a righteous man is powerful and effective" (James 5:16).

People of all races, creeds, and denominations have found prayer to be an effective solution to getting at the root of a problem, obtaining a Godly solution, or obtaining the strength needed to endure a situation. When one prays, they open up the lines of communication to God. People pray for a variety of reasons. Prayer is a petition to God for Him to hear us. Someone once asked me, "Are all prayers answered"? My response to that question was, "Yes." However, all prayers are not always answered in the time frame or in the manner the petitioner might want. What's key to remember is that God answers prayers according to His time, not ours.

Consequently, if you're considering marriage, you should know that God's response to your petition will be based on His timing and nothing less than His word. If your reason for marriage does not align with His principles, be ready to receive signs, signals, and warnings that all point to slowing down or not going through with the marriage. Friend, use God's response to your petition wisely. If there are things about you or your potential significant other that require correction before marriage, happily thank God for giving you the heads up needed to get those circumstances fixed.

Additionally, when you pray to God, you should be very

specific about your prayer request. It might be helpful to remember that God is most interested in having a relationship with us. As such, do not assume that just because He is God, He is not concerned with the most intricate details of our lives. You should know that God is most certainly interested in what you have to say. He wants to hear what comes from your heart and from your honesty. Over time, this exchange will create the connection that will allow you to receive and send messages from God without interruption.

Confession

2. The second step toward hearing God's voice is confession. Here's what the scripture says regarding confession:

    A. "If we confess our sins, he is faithful and just and will forgive us our sins and purify us from all unrighteousness" (1 John 1:9)

    B. "For it is with your heart that you believe and are justified, and it is with your mouth that you confess and are saved" (Romans 10:10).

Our second step toward hearing the voice of God requires a true recognition of sin and an understanding of the redemption efforts made by Jesus Christ to reconcile humanity to the Father. Therefore, if you are serious about hearing the voice of God, you must confess to Him that your life is nothing without His complete involvement in your life. Moreover, you must acknowledge that you deserve nothing less than judgment for your sins and that, without the precious blood of His son Jesus Christ, your soul would be cast into the lake of fire (Luke 16:23-24, Rev. 20:14) for all eternity. This step means that your heart, body, soul, and all are pliable for reproof and correction. It also means that you're receptive to His truths and principles for your life. Confession is critical in one's journey toward hearing God's voice and His instructions for our lives. If the goal is to be able to tune in to the frequency of God, prayer, and confession in combination are the equivalent of raising our spiritual antennas in preparation for receiving and downloading the transmission.

Our third step toward hearing the voice of God starts with being dedicated to effective biblical study. Of the four basic methods toward hearing the voice of God, this method can be the most difficult for a variety of reasons. First, there is the issue of time. Let's face it: our work schedules and daily activities sometimes make it difficult for us to steal away and spend some time alone studying God's word. Before you get discouraged, please understand that sin is not set up for knowing God but, rather, keeping you from knowing Him. Consequently, the inflexibilities of life are not designed to give humanity the freedom desired to devote regular daily consecration to the Almighty. You must set a specific time to devote to Christian education and biblical study.

"All Scripture is given by inspiration of God, and is profitable for doctrine, for reproof, for correction, for instruction in righteousness, that the man of God may be complete, thoroughly equipped for every good work."

2 Timothy 3:16-17

In the absence of knowledge about how to listen, how can we ever discern God's voice? One can hear God's voice as clearly as a bus passes by on the freeway or a fighter jet throttling overhead. Once a person has been exposed to wisdom, studied sacred scriptures, and applied the combination to their entire being, hearing the voice of the Creator is beyond easy. It's innate. In fact, it becomes as natural to an individual as breathing. And that is not an exaggeration.

The second thing that makes Biblical study difficult is the overabundance of false prophets. I'm sad to say this, but I must: false prophecy has become a billion-dollar industry in this country and worldwide. People, who are really in search of the truth, find themselves being taken advantage of year after year by false prophets promising to have unique or special gifts from God. These false prophets often convince misguided souls to seed money into their ministries by purchasing books, DVDs, or CDs. Each year, people by the hundreds of thousands travel far distances to attend "so-called" Christian conferences with the hope of finally hearing the voice of God. Friend, many of these "Jackleg Preachers and Televangelists" are nothing more than false prophets posing as men and women of God. Typically, these "pulpit rock stars" are nothing more than graduates of so-called schools of theology who have studied the Christian Bible to enter the profession of Church. In other words, these are men and women who have set out on a schedule very different than God's.

For years, false prophets, teachers, and so-called gospel performers, inspired by satanic influence, have taken advantage of God's people simply because God's chosen don't readily know His word or recognize His voice. A person can take complete advantage of you only when you're ignorant of what gives you the advantage. If you have a rare coin and know its true worth and value, no one can tell you that it's worth less than you know it to be. No matter how hard they try or how persuasive their argument is, you know the coin's value. It's the same way as knowing God's word. To know the true value of His word, you have to know it, be sure of it, and apply it. Therefore, regular devotion to biblical study is very important.

Several scriptures in the Bible tell us our efforts to seek God's word will not be easy, but if we search for His word, His truths, His standards, and His righteousness making that effort first, foremost, and paramount in our lives, our lives will indeed be in line with His word (Matthew 6:33). Subsequently, the totality of our lives and concerns will be of utmost importance to Him, and upon our return to Him after our time on Earth has ended, we will be welcomed home for our faithful service to Him. Hearing the voice of God means that our basis for study must be the Bible and the truths it contains. Moreover, our goal should be for God to reveal His truths to our hearts so that we may understand His perfect will for our lives.

All too often today, people are willing to bank their salvation solely on what is said by a preacher, taking everything they say to heart without accurately measuring whether what's being said is the truth or a tall tale. Again, our salvation is too important to leave to chance. This is vital if you are serious about hearing God's voice and being led by His principles and standards for your life. Hearing God's voice through His written Word can help you determine if what you desire for your life is what God desires for you.

Scripture reveals the following with regards to our examination of the text and the application of what we have learned to our lives:

"...be diligent to present yourself approved to God, a worker who does not need to be ashamed, rightly dividing the word of truth."

2 Timothy 2:15

The fourth basic method towards hearing the voice of God starts with having Godly counsel. An old expression: "Birds of a feather flock together." This expression tells us that birds of a particular flock or grouping stay within that group. In essence, you will never see an eagle soaring with a group of ducks. Are they both fowl of the air? Yes, they are. However, they are different types of fowl; they have different characteristics, abilities, purposes, and instincts. Subsequently, the eagle may view the duck as prey. Therefore, it's not in the duck's interest to be anywhere near an eagle, let alone flying in a group of them. It is the same for you and me in our journey to hearing the voice of God.

We must separate ourselves from those influences that prevent us from hearing His voice. What does this mean? It means that there is some folk in our lives that we may have to cut loose while moving closer to God. It also means that we must use prayer, confession, and biblical study to signal to God that we are now ready to be surrounded by people who are of like minds and thoughts.

Surrounding ourselves with Godly people and counsel doesn't make us separatist, nor does it mean that we are better than another group. It simply means that we are putting ourselves in the best position possible, combining like minds to form a oneness, purposed on being purpose-driven for God. The Bible tells us that iron sharpens iron (Proverbs 27:17). When we surround ourselves with people with a mind of righteousness, God uses those relationships to speak His words through people's heart to have them live their best in their trek toward everlasting life. Here's what the scripture says regarding biblical counsel:

"Where no counsel is, the people fall: but in the multitude of counselors there is safety."

2 Proverbs 11:14

Again, these are the four basic ways of hearing the voice of God. However, there are a variety of other methods. Here are just a few for your consideration:

- Surrender
- Journaling
- Meditation
- Visions, Dreams
- Messages of Knowledge & Wisdom
- Prophetic Revelations
- Inner Peace
- Worship
- Signs
- Discernment
- Fasting
- History
- Stories & Parables
- And many, many more

Friend, trust me when I say that you do not want to decide to get married based on an emotion, a whim, or even a terrific night of sex. You want the most serious decision one will ever make in a lifetime to line up with the principles of God. Again, having been down the marriage road, I know firsthand what happens when you don't pray, confess, study His word, and surround yourself with Godly counsel: you end up in divorce court.

Some people may say, "It doesn't take all of that to get married!" However, I say, people who rush into marriage without first getting an answer from God are people who are doomed to make the same mistakes in life over and over again. However, truly wise people seek His counsel every step of the way.

So, when it is all said and done, which person will you be? Are you willing to accept the wise counsel that has been offered to you? Or is it your intention to be the next plaintiff or defendant in divorce court? Ultimately, you are in charge of your decision.

CHAPTER 7 | **DEEP FACTS & TAKEAWAYS**

1. It is estimated that divorce rates are 76-95% higher when only one spouse smokes. When the spouse with the habit is the wife, the divorce rate increases significantly.

2. Even though couples who both smoke have a bit of an advantage over non-smoking couples, a 1998 study showed they are still 53% more likely to end their marriage than non-smoking couples.

3. Drinking one liter of alcohol per day increases your chances of divorce by 20%! In addition, the average American drinks 9.4 liters of alcohol every year, which increases their chances of divorce by 188%!

4. Researchers from the University of Buffalo have found that couples who share similar drinking patterns are more likely to remain together - whether they are both heavy drinkers or not.

RELATIONSHIP IQ | **INSIGHTFUL QUESTIONS**

- If your parents and I have a disagreement, whose side will you most likely take?

- Whom would you rather disappoint, your parents or me?

- Do your parents have a strong opinion on how you should live your married life?

- Do you foresee us living with either of our parents at any time during our married life?

- Is it more important to have a good relationship with your parents or me?

- Would you be willing to move to a location far away from your family?

- If your parents criticize our married lifestyle, how would you respond?

- How often to you speak with your parents?

- Regarding family and the holiday season, how do you envision spending the holidays, and with whom?

By wisdom a house is built, and by understanding it is established; by knowledge the rooms are filled with all precious and pleasant riches. A wise man is full of strength, and a man of knowledge enhances his might, for by wise guidance you can wage your war, and in abundance of counselors there is victory. Wisdom is too high for a fool; in the gate he does not open his mouth.

Proverbs 24:3-7

Chapter

8

CAN YOU
SAY "I DO" TO
BAD CREDIT

The thrill of the marriage proposal is just the beginning of two people uniting together as one. A huge part of this marital merger involves a couple's finances. Essentially, two separate systems of accounting must be brought together as one. Typically, couples tend to forget this important component when deciding to marry. Although the wedding day is important, it is, in fact, one day. According to the National Directory of Marriage and Family Counseling, the divorce rate in America has stayed around 50% since the mid-'80s. Since many of the divorces experienced in this country result from money-related matters, you need to know your financial situation before jumping the broom.

So, what is the first step in preparing for your financial merger? The first step involves knowing the financial strengths and weaknesses and your potential partner. To determine what your strengths and weaknesses are, the two of you will need to have some healthy discourse regarding the following:

1. How would you rank the following choices in importance? Using the numbers one through five, prioritize the following:

    a. _____ Getting out of debt?

    b. _____ Paying off a Mortgage?

    c. _____ Investing for retirement?

    d. _____ Establishing Savings (i.e. emergency)?

2. How much money would it be okay to spend without discussion?

3. Will you have separate or joint accounts?

4. Do you currently balance your checkbook?

5. Do you currently live on a written budget?

No matter what anyone may say about love conquering all or that money should not play a role in a relationship, money always plays a role. More than ever, if you want to have a successful marriage, you need a solid financial foundation. In an era where costs are rising, and employment opportunities are decreasing, you can hardly afford to be saddled by an individual that is not financially mature.

Long gone are the draconian days where one spouse is expected to carry the whole load. Ask any couple that went from being a two-income household to a one-income household how hard it is not just on the finances but in the impact that it often has on the relationship. Believe it or not, once-loving couples find themselves at odds because one is making the grade financially and the other spouse is not. If one spouse has only one income regardless of the circumstances that led to this situation, one spouse shouldering the burden often creates resentment in the spouse who is working against the spouse who is not.

Household finances can also be adversely affected by the following factors:

- Garnishments
- Wage liens
- Child support
- Tons of debt
- Bad credit

Together, these factors are enough to weaken the strongest marriages, especially in the case of unions that are based on needs rather than love. It is unethical to marry a man or woman with the intention of enriching oneself. Marriages conducted in the name of money rather than love are a disgrace to the institution of marriage and all of the individuals who entered into this most unique and sacred fraternity.

In all fairness to individuals that have married under similar circumstances, no one will ever know whether these unions were for love, for money, or the love of money. But in the age of internet influencers and reality television, we have learned that people will prostitute themselves to the highest bidders to obtain access to financial resources and some measure of security. Unfortunately, marriage has been historically used as an angle to this effort.

So, if you're considering marrying someone who does not have a solid financial footing, you should seriously consider whether now's a good time in your relationship to get married. Many of the factors that cause us financial difficulty will disappear. However, one factor will always loom large over our financials and our ability to secure financing, and that factor, my friend, involves credit.

If you're considering marriage, do you plan to stay with your parents or purchase your own home? How about transportation? Do you plan on purchasing your vehicle? How about credit cards? Do you plan on having a major charge card or credit card?

All of the items mentioned here are integral parts of our society today and play a fundamental role in marriages. I don't want to say that you can't have a winning marriage without credit, but I will say that not having access to credit can make marriage these days extremely difficult.

No one should ever enter into marriage without knowing that they are financially prepared and able to commit the financial resources necessary to support and sustain a marriage:

- Are you able to obtain credit?
- What is your credit rating?
- What is credit?
- Is it your intention to own a home or to rent an apartment?
- Are you planning to pay for your entire wedding with cash?
- What is the total amount of your debt? What type of debt do you have?
- In your marriage, how much debt and what kind of debt would be acceptable?

Friend, because you are not yet husband and wife, it is recommended that you not co-mingle your finances until you're married. Remember, your role as a "Love Investigator" is to determine if marriage to this person is right for you. So, before saying, "I DO!" I recommend that you do the following:

I. Be Clear About Your Short & Long-Term Financial Goals

- Write down your goals. Make them clear and use them throughout your marriage.

II. Implement Your Goals.

- If your marital goal is to purchase a home, you should begin working towards that personal goal. You can start by paying off individual debts or opening a savings account.

III. Create Individual Budgets.

- Each of you needs to have your budget. Creating a budget before marriage will give you a head start on the financial discipline, you'll need to achieve marital, financial success.

Even couples with equal financial means may find it challenging to establish a financial future together. When newlyweds have different credit histories, it can be difficult to combine their financial worlds.

So, if you have an excellent credit history and your spouse can't get a loan to buy a stick of gum, you need to know that their credit history can affect your perfect score. Therefore, you need to know how to protect your credit score while working to establish a credit history together.

Merged Credit Files

Your credit report and score are tied to your Social Security number. Consequently, your spouse's credit history will remain separate from yours and will not reflect your marital status. However, both credit reports will reflect the following:

- List accounts that you open together
- List accounts where one of you has cosigned for the other
- Addition of name to account as an authorized user

Get Full Disclosure Before Marriage

Many premarital counselors recommend that couples review their credit reports together before getting married. AnnualCreditReport.com offers free copies of your credit report from each of the three credit reporting agencies -- Equifax, Experian, and TransUnion.

Check your potential significant others report for things like:

- Late Payments
- High balances
- Collections
- Charge-offs
- Civil Judgements
- Bankruptcy
- Tax Liens
- Unpaid Student Loan(s)
- Foreclosures

DIG DEEP BEFORE YOU LEAP

If your spouse's credit report reveals high balances, unpaid debts, or another negative history, this may be a red flag that requires your attention. Although bad credit can be the product of a particular circumstance, it may be in your best interest to press the pause button on the nuptials until you can analyze their total financial picture. So, before saying, "I DO!" you may want to see whether you have the creditworthiness required to help make your marriage work.

Understanding Credit Scoring

In grade school, progress is measured by a grading system that uses letters of the English alphabet to denote one's progress:

- A = Excellent
- B = Above average
- C = Average
- D = Below average
- F = Failing

An instructor determines a student's letter grade using percentages from classwork, homework, exams, etc., along with a formula to calculate a student's scoring percentile. The final calculation or percentage is then aligned with the grade into which the percentage falls. Typically, a student's scoring or grade percentage is inserted between a scoring or grade range. For example, if it has been pre-determined that a scoring range of 90-100 translates to an "A" letter grade, a score of any number between 90 and 100 means that your letter grade is an "A." However, if you score below the 90-100 range, your score or grade range is compared with the next range until it is determined what your final grade is.

168

Likewise, the credit reporting agencies Equifax, Experian, and Trans Union use a model similar to the educational grading system to determine one's creditworthiness. However, the methodology used by each agency will vary depending on the formula or calculation used for determining an individual's credit score. Because of the different methodologies used, an individual's credit score may differ from one reporting agency to the next. For example, Experian may use the information contained within your credit report and determine that your credit score is 650. However, Equifax or Trans Union may examine the same information and calculate a different score based on their unique methodology.

Typically, the score between each agency differs only slightly. It's important to note that the methodologies used by Equifax, Experian, and Trans Union are proprietary. This means that the scoring methods used to calculate your credit score by each company are privately held trade secrets used by each company and not shared between companies or released to the general public.

Equifax uses the FICO credit-scoring model; Experian uses the Vantage Score scoring model, and Trans Union uses its Personal Credit Score scoring model. Each scoring model is unique. However, it stands for good reason that the scoring methodologies used by each credit agency were modeled after the FICO scoring model. FICO, which stands for Fair Isaac Company, uses a method in which the following aspects of one's credit report are examined:

- Payment history (35%)

- Amounts owed (30%)

- Length of credit history (15%)

- New credit (10%)

- Credit mix (10%)

Each of these (KEY) aspects is used to calculate one's total FICO score. Furthermore, each aspect is weighted by a numerical value that signifies the importance of each aspect. For example, out of 100 percentage points, your payment history or your ability to make timely payments to your creditors using the FICO model represents a value of 35 percent, while the outstanding balances or amounts owed using the same model hold a value of 30 percent. As you can see, your ability to meet your monthly obligations each month on time, along with the outstanding balances listed on your report, accounts for 65% of the total 100% using the FICO scoring system.

WHAT FACTORS MAKE UP YOUR CREDIT SCORE?

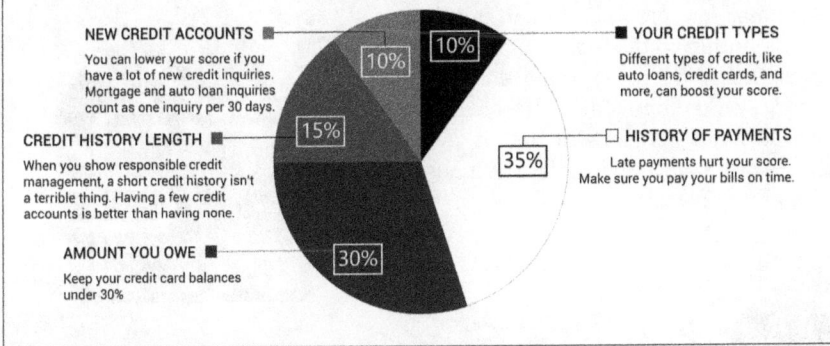

NEW CREDIT ACCOUNTS ■
You can lower your score if you
have a lot of new credit inquiries.
Mortgage and auto loan inquiries
count as one inquiry per 30 days.

CREDIT HISTORY LENGTH ■
When you show responsible credit
management, a short credit history isn't
a terrible thing. Having a few credit
accounts is better than having none.

AMOUNT YOU OWE ■
Keep your credit card balances
under 30%

YOUR CREDIT TYPES ■
Different types of credit, like
auto loans, credit cards, and
more, can boost your score.

HISTORY OF PAYMENTS ☐
Late payments hurt your score.
Make sure you pay your bills on time.

10% · 10% · 15% · 35% · 30%

Again, the scoring methodologies used by Equifax, Experian, and Trans Union may differ. However, your payment history, payments owed, length of accounts, various types of credit used, and attempts to establish new credit are key factors in any scoring model or system. Equally important, potential lenders examine these factors carefully when a credit request has been made.

Using the FICO scoring methodology, let's look at each of the key aspects used in determining one's creditworthiness by examining some real-life situations where a lender would review one's credit report.

Real life Situation #1

John has four credit cards and two charge cards on his credit report, of which three are older than seven years and the two charge cards are from the last two years. He also has a mortgage that is over 10 years old and three installment loans that are under five years in age.

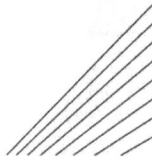

New Credit Accounts. This is certainly not an uncommon scenario. Let's face it: in our everyday lives, emergencies like this occur. It is 3:00 AM in the dead of winter and the furnace malfunctions. Perhaps it is summertime, and a lightning storm causes the neighbor's tree to fall in your living room.

As the Nationwide Insurance commercial suggests, "Life comes at you fast." Emergencies may require that you seek financial assistance from lending institutions as soon as possible. Whenever such situations occur, and credit is required, an application for credit must be completed.

Using the FICO scoring methodology, a "new credit request" creates a 10% hit against the cap of 100%. Requiring new credit from a lender has its rewards, but it can create severe drawbacks. Too many new requests for credit can kill a credit score. Furthermore, they can impact an individual's ability to secure the best rates or even a lender's credit approval. When requesting new credit, one should ensure that the same credit requests are not being made at different locations.

This type of behavior is certain to send up red flags in the lending community, as it says you're seeking credit from multiple sources, so maybe you're being turned down. This is common among people searching for a new car. I remember when I first entered the market for a new car; without any knowledge of the credit game, credit scores, or even the importance of having good credit, I went from car dealership to car dealership, completing application after application, and never once purchased the type of car I wanted, nor did I ever obtain or achieve a favorable interest rate.

The simple fact is that every application I completed for credit for the same item worked against my ability to obtain favorable credit rates and approval. A request for new credit creates an inquiry on your consumer credit report. An inquiry is an item on a consumer's credit report that shows that someone has previously requested a copy of the consumer's report. Based on the definition, can you imagine five different requests for credit occurring on the same day for the same type of item?

Knowing what you have learned thus far regarding credit, if you're Mr. Lender and this credit application is placed on your desk for approval, what would your answer be? If you said, "Credit application denied," that may be a bit drastic–but it's not impossible. I am trying to make a simple point: having too many inquiries is bad for business and WILL severely impact your ability to obtain favorable rates and possibly the lender's credit approval–period.

Through wisdom a house is built, and by understanding it is established; and by knowledge the rooms shall be filled with all precious and pleasant riches."

Proverbs 24:3-4

Helpful Hints:

- Secure financing through one lending source.

- Creating too many inquiries on your credit report is bad for business.

- Limiting your application to no more than two lending sources lessens the impact of a lender's inquiry on your credit report.

- Examine your credit report periodically before completing a new credit application. There may be issues that could adversely affect your chances of obtaining a favorable rate or receiving the lender's approval.

Real life Situation #2

The loan application for Lori and Douglas has been submitted to Ransom Bank for approval. Douglas' credit history includes three installment loans, five revolving accounts, a fixed mortgage loan, two credit cards and two charge cards.

Types of Credit. Using the FICO scoring methodology, the "types of credit used" portion of one's credit report holds a value of 10% of the total 100% of the report. When a lender reviews your credit report to determine whether credit can be extended on your behalf, various questions must be answered.

However, there is no question more important than whether you can pay back the loan. Examining your credit report to see what types of credit have been used helps a lender make this determination. Typically, a lender examines your credit report to see the total number of accounts and the active types of accounts.

The FICO scoring methodology uses a calculation or formula that compares your amount of debt to your available spending limit. This calculation or formula takes into consideration the types of credit obtained. Typically, a consumer report with a mixture of different credit product types, such as fixed payment or installment loans, revolving lines of credit, and mortgages, is certain to increase one's credit score. Moreover, it will prove invaluable in securing approval for a bank loan.

However, when establishing the right mixture of accounts, you need to make sure you do not have too many accounts, as this may alert a lender with a red flag. In other words, having too many active revolving accounts may send the message that a credit application may be over-extended, which means that one does not have enough cash flow to meet all of one's monthly obligations. This type of situation is a credit score killer.

Real life Situation #3

While Tina and Michael are traveling to a concert, their car breaks down. They decide to purchase a new car when they determine that the engine is blown and the repair costs will be more than the car's actual value.

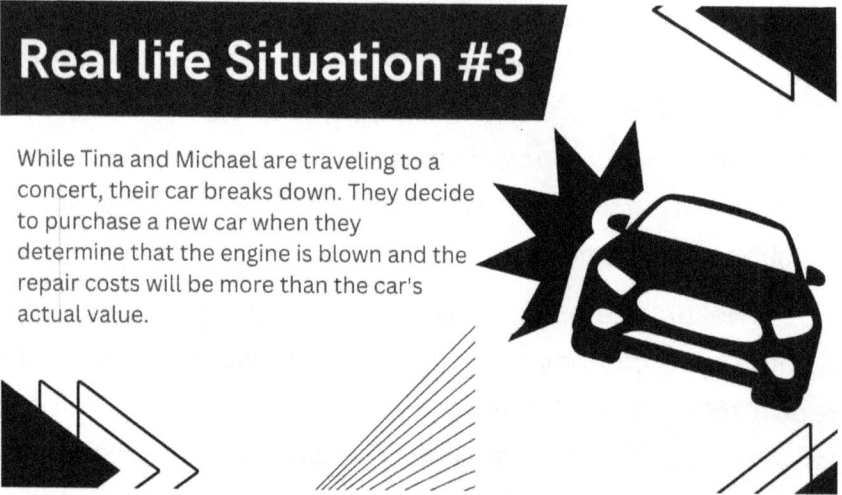

Length of Credit History. Established lines of credit speak volumes to potential lenders and have a huge impact on your credit score. If we look at our example, we see that Steve has had three major credit cards for more than seven years. The history tied to each of these credit cards can impact his credit report positively or negatively. Using the FICO scoring methodology, we see that the "length of credit history" portion of one's credit report accounts for 15% of the report. Having no credit history on your credit report is a negative since lenders use your credit history to determine your creditworthiness.

In some cases, no history can be as bad as negative history. If your history shows that your accounts have been frequently delinquent, this WILL hurt your ability to secure credit. Managing your established lines of credit by making your payments on time, keeping your current cards active, never using more than 40% of your account balance, and making payment for the amount used by the due date WILL increase your score and show creditors you're able to manage your credit matters well.

Amounts Owed. Several passages of scripture in the Bible discuss lending and borrowing principles. One scripture admonishes one to be the lender and not the borrower. Proverbs 22.7 says, "The rich rules over the poor, and the borrower is servant to the lender." Psalms 37:21 teaches us that "the wicked borrows and does not repay." There are multiple refrains of truth in each one of these passages. However, there is no greater truth than the one that screams to each of us to be responsible and pay our debts. This truth is important to God and the individuals to whom we have become indebted.

In light of this, this aspect of your credit report is extremely important. When calculating your credit score, 30% of the value is attributed to the amount you owe. The impact of this section on your ability to obtain credit is significant. Your lender's decision about whether or not to grant you credit is clearly determined by this factor. Creditors evaluate your repayment ability by reviewing the "amounts owed" section of your credit report. A creditor typically considers the number of accounts with no balance, the balance remaining on revolving credit lines, consistent payments, and outstanding installment loan balances.

Your Payment History. Finally, using the FICO scoring methodology, we see that the "payment history" portion of one's credit report accounts for 35% of the report. This portion of your credit report carries a higher number than any other aspect of your credit report. This means that creditors are paying close attention to your payment history. Your ability to repay a loan tells credit lenders whether you are credit-worthy or a risk. As an example, if Steve is the type of customer who fulfills his online credit obligations each month without late payments, keeps his credit card balance 30%-50% below the spending limit, pays more than the minimum amount due each month, and monitors his credit report and score frequently, he is sure to establish the type of credit score that financial institutions prefer to see. In summary, if you are considering getting married, credit is either an asset or a liability depending on your situation. How is your credit?

What are your credit and financial situation? What is the creditworthiness of the person you're considering marriage to? Is their credit good, bad, or non-existent? If you are unsure, it's probably a good idea to review credit reports and scores to see where you are financially before walking down that aisle. Remember to pay close attention to the new accounts, various types of credit used, length of credit history, outstanding balances/debts owed, and payment history sections of your credit report. These areas are critical to making a true assessment of your creditworthiness.

Remember, no matter which scoring model, methodology, or credit-reporting agency is used, lenders examine these key areas to determine whether you're creditworthy or a credit risk. Again, many marriages fail, in part, due to financial problems or the inability to obtain credit. No matter how strong your love tie or bond is with your potential significant other, wisdom says it's better to repair the hole in the boat while it's on dry land than to make repairs while it's sinking. If you're indeed considering marriage, it will serve you well to make issues related to financial matters, particularly credit, a part of your decision-making process.

CHAPTER 8 | **DEEP FACTS & TAKEAWAYS**

1. It is estimated that couples with one spouse who is a heavy drinker and the other who is not are 60 percent more likely to get divorced.

2. Based on the findings of a multi-national study published in 2011, eighteen different mental disorders all increased the likelihood of divorce - ranging from a 20 percent increase to an 80 percent increase. Addictions and major depression were the most significant factors, followed by PTSD (Post-Traumatic Stress Disorder).

3. Nearly 15 percent of divorcing couples cited video game addiction as a major reason for their divorce.

4. In the United States, 43 percent of children are being raised without their fathers.

5. There is a 14 percent reduction in divorce risk among children whose parents are happily married.

RELATIONSHIP IQ | **INSIGHTFUL QUESTIONS**

- Have you ever declared bankruptcy?
- Would you consider declaring bankruptcy in the future?
- Do you know your current FICO score?
- Is your credit in good standing overall?
- Are you currently in debt?

- Do your parents pay any of your current expenses?

- Would you be willing to accept financial assistance from your parents after we get married?

- Are you currently in debt to any friends?

- Do you prefer to pay cash for things, or do you prefer to use credit cards? Are you currently saving any money?

- At what time of the month do you save money?

- Does your company match your 401(k) contributions?

- Are you involved in your company's 401(k) match program?

"There is no fear in love. But perfect love drives out fear because fear has to do with punishment. The one who fears is not made perfect in love."

1 John 4:18 (NIV)

Chapter

9

MARRIAGE AFTER DIVORCE

When a person decides to remarry, they tend to bring their baggage or, should I say, past marital experiences along for the ride, so before you say, "I DO!", I need you to consider a couple of questions. First, did you learn anything from your previous relationship? If so, what did you learn? The answers to both of these questions are important to your future marital success. Again, having experienced the snare of divorce, I know firsthand the true power of learning from past relationship experiences. So, with that said, if you're not willing to learn from your failures, it is more likely that you will repeat them, and, unfortunately, that's exactly what happens to most people entering into marriage a second time. Because of this reality, many people pass on the idea of remarriage altogether. Still, if they decide to wed again, they do it with a great deal of trepidation, as the anxiety associated with a second possible failed marriage is always in their minds. Therefore, regardless of where you might fall in this equation, you need to know that you can find true love and happiness after divorce, but you will need to do a couple of things.

Accept Your Role In Your Divorce

First, to move on to your new life after divorce, you must take and accept full responsibility for your role in the divorce itself. People often like to blame their failed marriage on the ex-spouse. However, there is no circumstance in which both parties don't share an equal part of the blame. Even if your role in the marriage's demise is minimal, it's still your role.

Taking responsibility for your actions is the biggest step toward not repeating the same mistakes. Likewise, you're willing to learn from your past failures rather than turn a blind eye to them.

Resolve Previous Marital Matters

In addition to accepting your role, you must also resolve all matters associated with your previous marriage. There is nothing worse than entering into a second marriage with baggage from the first. Therefore, you must create a clean break between your past and your future by settling all matters related to your previous experience.

This may include matters related to:

- Finances
- Custody
- Property

- Past-due bills
- Loans
- Mortgage

It's also equally important that you make sure to resolve any emotional issues related to your past relationships. If you haven't quite resolved past hurts or transgressions, you may want to consider individual counseling or therapy to help with your lingering issues. Keep in mind that this counseling should not be a part of premarital counseling but, rather, individual counseling to help you deal with your past emotions. If you consider remarriage and carrying emotional baggage, therapy is an absolute must.

Identify Your Strengths and Weaknesses

What strengths can you point to in your first marriage to help you in your new union? Were you a good listener? Were you a good team player or good with the finances? You must identify those things about you that will help make your new marriage a success. Likewise, it's equally important for you to identify areas of weakness. For example, let's say that you're lousy when managing finances. This is an opportunity for you to either improve that skillset or be willing to cede control over the finances to your new partner if this area is their strength. Remember, the idea of marriage is the two of you becoming one, so, through your union, your weaknesses are made strong. Therefore, if you have an area of weakness that contributed to your first marriage's demise, you may consider checking that flaw.

Discover Your Partner

If you're talking about marriage again, you should seriously consider your decision. It's not enough to think that you have gathered all the facts; you must know that you have gathered them. You must get to know your new spouse on a very deep and intimate level. If you refuse to follow this step, you will be in line again at the courthouse to sever ties because of a bad decision.

Transparency

To find true love, you must be willing to expose yourself to the vulnerability that true love often yields. What does this mean? If you're expecting to find happiness in remarriage, you must be willing to be open and honest about your hopes, dreams, wishes, concerns, fears, and expectations. To have true marital success, you must be willing to share yourself completely without the fear of failure, hurt, or judgment.

Premarital Counseling

Once you have resolved in your spirit to become transparent, it's time for you and your spouse to attend premarital counseling. If you avoided premarital counseling the first time around, you could not afford to avoid this step now. Likewise, if this is a second marriage for your potential spouse, premarital counseling is an absolute must. Regarding premarital counseling, if either you or your new partner elects to skip this step, consider this a "red flag" and do not move forward with any discussions of marriage until premarital counseling is accepted for certain, not for pretend.

Counseling Motivation

You're probably asking, "What do you mean by for certain and not pretend?" Well, some people go through premarital counseling to appease their partner. As a result, they are not fully engaged or vested in the benefits that premarital counseling offers. This is not the marital partner you want or the partner you want to be, so if you're talking remarriage, you'd better be talking remarriage counseling even if you had marriage counseling before.

Cleaning the Slate

Another step toward remarriage success involves cleaning the slate. Typically, people who marry a second time have homes, neighborhoods, and familiar settings associated with the previous marriage. It would help if you broke free from the old stomping grounds of your past. If your favorite sit-down restaurant was a place for you and your former spouse to break bread, it's time for you to identify some new eateries for you and your new love. In your new relationship, your role is to create new beginnings, not recreate your past, so don't allow the memories of yesterday to impact your future blessings.

Create New Habits

Whenever a new chapter begins, it is essential to start with a clean slate. If, during your first marriage, you only washed clothes on Saturdays, consider creating a new habit of doing laundry during the week so you can spend Saturdays with your spouse. As well, if you previously spent holidays with your former spouse with mutual friends, you may wish to consider spending future holidays with new acquaintances that you have made together. Remarrying successfully requires the creation of new habits and traditions, as this prevents the worlds of the past and present from colliding.

Learn To Be Flexible

Speaking of habits, people who have been divorced and single for a while getting into a rhythm of not having to answer to anyone. These people have become used to the following:

- Unrestrained spending
- Bill payment practices
- Socializing
- Late nights
- Vacationing
- Cooking rarely

If you have been divorced for any time, you know exactly what I am talking about. Therefore, you must learn to be flexible when it comes to remarriage. Yes, it is very difficult to break old habits. However, if you're committing to do things the right way, it sometimes means having to bend but not break. Instead of spending time with friends every weekend, you designate a particular time to hang out each month. You're probably saying, "I'm grown. I don't have to ask permission to go out." Well, this is not about asking for permission. It's about respecting the institution of marriage and the partner you agree to spend the rest of your life with. Here's what's important to remember: in every divorce throughout the annals of time, the underlining reason for the divorce involved inflexibility. It was the inflexibility of one party, the other party, or both. If you're considering doing this thing called marriage again, are you willing to commit to the idea of flexibility? Are you willing to commit to the principle of "bend, not break," which means that a person's willingness to be flexible does not mean that they are willing to be broken? Finally, are you flexible enough to change?

Remarriage Motive

If you're flexible enough to change, that is good. However, if your willingness to change a certain habit or behavior is driven by a fear of being single and alone, you are ensuring a terrible decision. Your reason for getting married should not be driven by a fear of anything, particularly loneliness. However, if this is your reason for getting married, you will inevitably end up alone because your fear will eventually strangle your new beginning. The person you're with will say, "It's been real, but I'm out." Thus, you will be left with another failed marriage on your resume, so if you're committing to remarry, make it based on love, not fear.

According to statistics on how many people remarry after divorce, I have discovered a few facts that I believe are invaluable. First, if you have had the misfortune of being divorced, statistics suggests that you will indeed remarry again? Yep! It is very likely that you will remarry if you have experienced a divorce. Even though the first thought after a divorce might be "never again," statistics on remarriage after divorce demonstrate that roughly 70% of people who get divorced will subsequently get married again at some point in their lives. How soon you can remarry after divorce, well that depends on what state you live. Depending on your state, there might be a waiting period. Most states do not impose a waiting period for remarriage after a divorce, however, there are a few states that have such a law.

In my view, a waiting period should be imposed whether your state has one or not. If you've been divorced, you should avoid getting into a second marriage right away. Divorce is an emotionally draining process that takes time to work through. Remarrying after divorce statistics show that "about half of all people who experience a divorce will remarry within 5 years of a divorce, a figure that has been decreasing by 10% for several decades."

Of course, everyone is different, but remarriage after divorce statistics show that "about half of all people who experience a divorce will remarry within 5 years of a divorce." Prior to remarrying, it is recommended that you consult an attorney.

The legal restrictions regarding remarriage are few, but they do exist. Your lawyer can help you identify these restrictions. The decrees of some divorces will affect remarriage, so if your new fiancé is divorced, he or she will need to discuss those legal considerations with you. Additional issues that may affect your second marriage include alimony, child support, custody, and inheritance provisions that may impact the distribution of your estate to your children.

If you are currently divorced, and you haven't done so already, it is definitely recommended that you consider therapy. This will go a long way in helping you to heal from the experience of a failed marriage. Additionally, to avoid a second divorce, you should consider therapy, and premarital counseling and investigation. If you're curious about the second marriage divorce rate, approximately 15% end within three years and 25% end within five years. As such, therapy can be the key factor in lowering the divorce rate of second marriages.

Stephanie Coontz, the author of Marriage, a History: How Love Conquered Marriage and The Way We Never Were; American Families and the Nostalgia Trap, is quoted as saying,

"They need to have some good conversations with each other – and themselves – about what they contributed to the failure of their first marriage and what they saw as problems in their first partner that they would like to avoid the second time around. In other words, the process of re-evaluating, stepping away from the anger, blame, disappointment and self-righteousness that often come with the first emotional responses to divorce. They have to analyze what they need to do differently this time if they want to succeed."

To that end, it is important to not rush it and to take your time. And speaking of time, have you taken a moment to consider what a second marriage might mean to your children? If you have kids, some consideration must be given to how a second marriage might affect there well-being. After finding peace within yourself, you have decided that you are ready to find the one. However, your children may be experiencing a range of different emotions in regard to their parents remarrying. Even though it is rare for parents to reunite, children often hope that their parents will do so in the future. In order for them to heal and cope with the reality that their parents are seeking new partners; they will require sufficient time.

Provide them with a reasonable amount of time to process their emotions and do not introduce them to your partners unless you are seriously considering that person as a long-term partner. For children, meeting new prospective stepparents and having that person leave their lives can be an emotional roller coaster. It is in your best interest, your children, and your new relationship to take the relationship slowly. Before giving marriage another chance, it is important to decide if you and your partner are ready to work on it together. The odds may not be in your favor. It is also necessary to address the characteristics that impede long-term relationship success before committing to another marriage.

Recognizing what went wrong in the first marriage is fundamental to a successful remarriage. While many people blame their problems on their ex-partner after a divorce, being realistic about your own role in the failure of the relationship is necessary for future relationships to succeed. Consider your own role in the breakup of your first marriage and take an objective look at what caused it to fail. You may have not been emotionally prepared for marriage in the past. Perhaps you struggled with anger or financial difficulties. Chances are if you haven't made any efforts to change the things that negatively impacted your previous relationships, your next relationship won't be any better.

How to Know Whether You're Ready to Remarry

The following are red flags that indicate either your partner or you are not ready to remarry:

- Despite being estranged from your former spouse, you still fantasize about getting back together.
- Perhaps you are angry about your ex-spouse and the divorce.
- It is difficult for you to be honest with your new partner.
- There are differences between your goals and values.

Nevertheless, the fact that you are not yet ready for remarriage does not mean that it should not be considered in the future. This is where therapy really has value. You can gain a clearer picture of the issues that brought about your first divorce by working with a mental health professional individually or as a couple. In my view, therapy is a useful tool for anyone considering marriage. As well as helping you build trust and clear communication with your current partner, they can pave the way for a long-lasting and healthy relationship.

CHAPTER 9 | **DEEP FACTS & TAKEAWAYS**

1. Divorce in the United States costs an average of $15,000.

2. In families with children that were not poor before the divorce, incomes can fall by as much as 50 percent.

3. After a divorce, nearly half of the parents with children move into poverty.

4. Two-thirds of newly divorced women had less than $25,000 in household income, compared to one-third of recently divorced men.

5. In the United States, 60% of people living in poverty are divorced women and children.

RELATIONSHIP IQ | **INSIGHTFUL QUESTIONS**

- Do you want children? If so, when, and how many?

- Are you able to have children?

- How would you feel if we were unable to have children?

- What would you do if there were an accidental pregnancy before we planned to have children?

- Who is responsible for birth control?

- Would you consider adoption if you were unable to have a child naturally?

- What is your view of abortion?

- Should a husband have an equal say in whether his wife has an abortion?

- Have you ever had an abortion?

- Have you ever given birth to a child or fathered a child who was put up for adoption?

- How important is it to you that your children are raised near your extended family?

- Do you believe in spanking a child?

- What type of discipline do you believe in?

- Do you believe that children should have a foundation based on Christian principles?

- In a blended family, should birth parents be in charge of making decisions for their own children?

- How do you feel about home schooling?

Behold, children are a heritage from the LORD, the fruit of the womb a reward. Like arrows in the hand of a warrior are the children of one's youth. Blessed is the man who fills his quiver with them! He shall not be put to shame when he speaks with his enemies in the gate.

Psalm 127:3-5

Chapter

10

STEPPING UP TO
STEPPARENTING

n today's society, most new marriages involve children from previous relationships. Suppose you and your potential spouse have decided to build a new life together and create a new family consisting of children from one or both of your previous relationships. In that case, you may want to consider the rewards and challenges this new union may bring. Unfortunately, what's lost in the excitement of the two participants tying the knot is the emotional impact of the new marriage and blended family. Where there may be a big joy for the new husband and wife, there could be pure misery for the children of these newly blended families.

Much of the anxiety comes from children's uncertainty regarding their place or standing in the relationship, not to mention their concerns about eventual changes and how they will affect their day-to-day interactions with their biological parents. If you consider marriage and blending your households, have you stopped to consider how the new siblings will react to one another now that you all reside under the same roof? What's the pecking order for responsibility related to children the same age? What if your children don't know each other well? While you were in this courtship period with your potential significant other, were your children being exposed to their kids and for that matter, their new grandparents, uncles, aunts and other members of the family?

If not, you may want to consider allowing these relationships to grow and blossom before saying, "I DO!" Kids tend to hide their resentment regarding these marriages and their feelings of betrayal and sometimes anger at the fact that a new stepmother or stepfather is being rammed down their throat. So, if you want to give your new marriage and family the best shot at happiness, you should start planning how a blended family will operate before getting married.

Blended Family Ground Rules

I can tell you from experience that people who manage to find love after divorce often rush into remarriage and blended family situations without ever really counting the costs of considering the need for creating the solid foundation needed for the new blended family's ultimate success. The best and safest advice is to take your time and do it right. Allow everyone involved an opportunity to get adjusted to one another and your new marriage. This is especially true for children. They are still children as fantastic, wonderful, and mature as your children are, and too much change can be very unsettling. If you want the best success in your new marriage and blended family, wait two years before tying the knot.

You shouldn't expect your partner's children to fall in love with you overnight, nor should you expect the happiest of receptions from their children. It's important to remember that your relationship with your potential spouse wasn't made overnight; it took a great deal of time to build. So, it would help if you put in the work to create a good relationship, rapport, and loving bond with your new stepchildren.

Remember, real and meaningful love is not established instantly; it's established over time. As a couple, you and your potential spouse can help to create these bonds and lasting memories together simply by finding real-life experiences you all can share. It would help if you considered taking all the children on outings to the park or zoo. You might also want to take them all to movies or pizza nights. Whatever the activity, choose outings that will be fun, enjoyable, and exciting and create the types of lasting memories that create family ties. In a perfect world, blended families get along amazingly well. But in the real world where you and I live, we know that things are not always picture-perfect, which brings me to my next point.

The parents of these blended families should expect push-back from the children involved in these marriages. You are likely to hear:

- "I don't have to do what you say! You're not my real mother/father!"

- "I know who my real mother/father is, and you are not it!"

These types of remarks are commonplace. However, it's critically important that you and your partner establish common rules, expectations, boundaries, and limits regarding the governance of your children. No hard and fast rule applies to all relationships, so it's up to you and your potential spouse to determine how discipline will be handled. However, it would help if you insisted on respect regardless of which action you and your potential spouse take. Therefore, conversations regarding discipline and child-rearing should be discussed before marriage.

The rules of action and discipline need to be clearly defined before your wedding day. Will, your new spouse, have the authority to discipline (i.e., spank) your children, or will you be the only one to dole out butt-whippings? Again, this needs to be discussed before marriage.

The outcome of your conversation needs to create between you and your new spouse a unified front that says to all the children involved that you are one and what one says is said for both, comes from both, and applies to both sets of children whether they live under the same roof full-time or not. Moreover, it would help if you protected your spouse. If you hear one of your children saying something off-color or disrespectful, jump dead on them and reinforce your rule that they will respect your spouse. Let them know that you understand and respect their feelings.

However, it's important that they maintain the utmost respect despite their feelings. Remember, disrespect from a child, regardless of their feelings, is unacceptable. Here's the bottom line: if you provide your children with the right support, they will come around to the idea of your getting married. Moreover, they will accept having a new family. Remember, it's your role as the adult to communicate openly, honestly, and effectively to dispel any concerns or trepidations they may feel and provide them with the security they are looking for in this new change in life's circumstances.

Blended Family Success

Your new blended family's success will rely heavily on your not attempting to recreate your first family. Doing so only leads to frustration, disappointment, and confusion. Rather than charting this course of action, the best action to take is to allow the new family to be just that—a new family. Learn to accept the differences, live life forward, and create new memories and enjoyable moments with your new children. Some essentials should be recognized for your new family to realize real success.

Rock Solid Marriage

Let's keep it real: there would be no need to discuss a new blended family if you were not considering getting remarried. Therefore, you must strike a balance between couple time and parenting time. This is often much harder in the second marriage than in the first, so you must devote time to building, maturing, and cultivating your marital relationship and fostering its success while parenting your children.

Marital and Family Civility

The lines of communication must remain open. There should be an open-door policy for everyone involved in the new blended family. Keeping the lines of communication open beats back the need or tendency for family members to ignore the concerns of other family members, which often creates negative feelings and emotions.

Open Lines of Communication

How you communicate as a family speaks to the success of your new blended family. Therefore, the following rules must be established in your new household regarding how you talk and interact with one another:

- Be respectful to each other.
- Approach conflict positively.
- Create a non-judgmental space or an atmosphere for open dialogue.
- Create family outings or activities.
- Be honest in communication.

Mutual Respect

Since everyone in this new family is new to each other, there will be some differences in how things are done. Also, there may be some challenges in how things are perceived or received. It's important to maintain healthy mutual respect for those differences. Again, it's equally important to have conversations regarding these differences if they create a problem or foster a bad attitude or emotion in one or more family members.

Human Expansion

Traditional married couples benefit from starting from scratch and growing together with their new families. Blended families have the challenge of incorporating children in different age groups with different attitudes and philosophies and working through those challenges to create a real family. It's important during this process that we allow the role of human expansion or development to occur. Different family members will have different needs; children, in most cases, will be in different stages of life. Therefore, family members need to understand, honor, and nurture those differences.

We Are Family

If these essential governing principles are followed, you will realize the awesome power of a fully operational family; you will see bonds forged between blended family members and, soon, see the "step" designations removed and replaced with "father," "mother," "brother," and "sister." This is the sweet spot of success for any blended family and truly the mark every blended family should strive for. You can proudly say, "We are family," and mean it when it's all said and done.

Parental Bonds

As a new parent by marriage, you need to create and develop relationships with your new kids. Before saying, "I DO!" give some thought to how you would develop this relationship; take some time to consider what the child or children may need and ask yourself the important question: "Am I really up to the challenge of raising someone else's child?" If you are up to the challenge, remember that children have some fundamental needs that should be addressed if you want to create a win-win relationship. Your role as a new parent by marriage is to make your new children feel:

- Safe and Secure
- Loved
- Valued
- Connected
- Appreciated
- Governance

Safety and Security

In most cases, stepchildren have already experienced the letdown of divorce and their nuclear family experience. The last thing any child needs is another scenario in which they're along for the ride but not a part of the experience. Your job as the new parent is to create a safe and secure environment that fosters behavior that allows your children to be all they can be within the freedom and liberty provided by the new family and the family's love experience.

Loved

Children need love, warmth, tenderness, and affection, but they don't need it all overnight. Kids today are a lot smarter than we often give them credit for. Trust me when I say that today's children know when you are giving them a wholesale snow job. In short, they can see through the BS, especially older or teenage children, so your feelings must be true and not contrived. Being fake with real emotions will cause more problems than being just true to yourself and the children. Real emotions and feelings will develop over time like anything else in life.

Real Value

Do you know what it's like to feel unimportant or irrelevant? Have you ever wanted to be chosen for something but weren't? Kids often feel this way in the traditional nuclear family. They often feel that their opinions are not important or that how they feel is not respected. Can you imagine what this must be like for a stepchild? It would help if you let your new children know that they are integral members of TEAM FAMILY and that their feelings and opinions are important, and that the success of your family strongly hinges on their involvement. Again, these feelings must be sincere and true to realize the best outcome.

Emotional Connections

It's equally important that children feel an emotional connection to and for their new parents. This is also created through openness, honesty, and a real avenue for dialogue. Some of the best parent-child relationships come from non-biological relationship situations involving second marriages.

Appreciation

These relationships are built through genuine feelings and a real sense of appreciation from both the parent's and children's sides of the spectrum. Let's be honest: kids love to be praised just as much as they hate being scolded, so heap on the appreciation when it's rightly deserved; let your children know what a wonderful job they did at this thing or that thing. Trust me: this will help build their confidence in themselves and establish love, respect, and trust in you.

Governance

When it comes to establishing rules and guidelines for your children to follow, their love, respect, and trust in you will be challenged. It's important to remember that it's not because of you but because you stand in the place of authority. It's the authority that they have a real problem with, not you, so when they say hurtful things such as, "You are not my real father, mother or biological parent," decide and declare openly that you have every expectation that they will do exactly what you say or reap the consequence of their disobedience. Remember, you must be fair, but it is equally important to be firm. It would help if you governed your natural children and your stepchildren from the same well of fairness. If you fail to do so, you will lose the power and respect of all the children for whom you're responsible.

About Blended Families

There are many types and sizes of blended families. There may be a child from a previous relationship between you and your partner, or one of you may be new to parenting. Your children may be of the same age or very different in age. You may also have a child together. Similarly, the place where children reside varies from family to family. It is possible that some children will live with you most or all of the time, while others may visit only occasionally. Some children have different living arrangements, for example, a teenager may spend most of his time with his father, whereas his younger brother may spend most of his time with his mother.

Blended Family Benefits

Being part of a new family has many benefits. For instance:

- You and your child can benefit from connecting with more individuals as you expand your extended family. Bringing step-grandparents into the lives of children can enrich their lives and make them feel loved even more.

- Blended families can be enjoyable. A variety of personalities, interests, and perspectives can be introduced to the family.

- Children and their parents may gain a great deal of support from stepparents and step-grandparents.

- Blended families often enable their children to connect with a wider range of people, so they become more flexible and tolerant.

Blended Family Challenges

Blended families face the same challenges as any other family. Being a member of a blended family takes some getting used to. In a blended family, the first two years are spent adjusting to the new family and building relationships. Establishing boundaries and rules for your blended family can also be challenging. Often, this is due to the fact that the families are coming together from different backgrounds and because everyone is still getting to know one another.

After memorializing your new romance, your relationship with your former partner may go through a difficult time because he or she might feel angry, insecure, upset, or worried about the change. Depending on your new family arrangements, you may need to adjust your co-parenting agreement. To that end, it is important to note that approximately 66% of second marriages involving children from previous marriages end in divorce. Stress, which is experienced by all members of a recently blended family, may play a role in this. It is common for newly blended families to be stressed. The transition may appear to have been handled smoothly. However, there is often a degree of stress. "Blended families" may imply a smooth transition. However, there may be difficulties in the early years.

Getting used to living together can take time for both families. There are many reasons for this, such as:

- Different parenting styles and discipline methods
- Development of meaningful relationships
- Feelings of conflict or tension

It is possible for everyone to have these challenges even if they never lived together before. Getting used to the new roles they have in the family may be difficult for the couple. Stepparenting may be difficult for one or both of the adults. There may also be tension in the relationship due to issues with the stepchildren. Some common challenges for couples in blended families include:

Being a new parent in a blended family. Not every adult in a blended family has children of their own. As stepparents, they will assume the role of parents for the first time. The transition can be stressful. Starting a romantic relationship can be challenging. Being liked by a stepchild while parenting them can be difficult. It can take time to adjust to being a parent. Additionally, gaining a partner's children's acceptance may take some time.

Interactions between stepparents and ex-partners. Many people choose to focus on finding a romantic partner after an old relationship ends. It can mean ceasing to communicate with the former partner. When children are involved, this can be more complicated. Biological (or first) parents may want their children to stay close to them. The child could be ordered to spend time with each parent under a court-ordered parenting plan. Remarried parents may need to continue to communicate with their former partners Ex-spouses may be referred to as non-resident parents in blended families.

Contact between their partner and their ex-lover can be perceived as a threat by some people. In other cases, the non-residential parent feels that their children are being unfairly treated by their stepparent. These are all situations that can increase tension in blended families. The difficulty of adjustment may be exacerbated by strained relationships.

Blended Families Present Multiple Challenges to Children

Change can also be stressful for children, especially older children. There may be more stress when there are more changes. Children usually suffer the most when they join a blended family. Their parents have already experienced a divorce. They then have to adjust to a new parent and its rules. It is possible that they may express their frustration in behavioral or emotional ways.

- **A stepchild's relationship with their stepparent.** Stepparents may cause children to have difficult feelings. Maybe they are accustomed to treating their parents' partner as a friend. This dynamic can change when the family becomes blended. The child may become resentful when their "friend" assumes the role of parent. It may appear that their new parent is trying to "replace" their other parent.

- **Stepparents may also face difficulties in gaining the trust of their children.** After a divorce, they may feel abandoned by their biological parent. When a child begins to care for their stepparent, they may experience new emotions. There may be concerns that love for the stepparent will betray their biological parent.

- **Stepchildren's relationship with their siblings.** A new dimension can also be added to the concept of sibling rivalry. In the newly formed household, children may feel they must compete for attention and dominance. Children may also be concerned that their biological parents may begin to favor their stepsiblings. Stepsiblings may similarly be subjected to bullying by their peers. This may be more prevalent for children who are competitive or insecure.

- **Visitation & Parental Arrangements.** There may also be difficulties associated with visiting the other parent. Children are accustomed to spending unstructured time with their parents each day. It is possible for parental plans to reduce the amount of spontaneity and flexibility in a child's life. The collapse of structures that the child has become accustomed to may cause stress.

- **Visits can be confusing.** Scheduling conflicts may lead to tension. Getting used to new family members can take some time. In addition, children may complain about their stepparent to their non-residential parents. Parents who have separated may already be experiencing tension in their relationship, and this may aggravate the issue.

- **Divorce leads to a sense of loss and grief.** Grief can also be present during the transition. Following the death of one parent, a remarriage may take place. In this scenario, the child may still be grieving the loss of the other parent. In addition, the child may also grieve the loss of their old family dynamics. A remarriage could further trigger these symptoms. Children may require additional time and space in order to grieve effectively. This will allow them to come to terms with the new parent at their own pace.

After some time has passed and things begin to settle, something amazing happens. The blended family begins to look, feel, and operate as a nuclear family. For this reason, a number of blended families would rather refer to themselves as a family. All children are referred to as brothers and sisters rather than half-siblings or stepsiblings. This is also true for the parental figures of the union as they are given the distinction of Mom or Dad, and they are referred to and introduced in that way. While others in society may describe your assembly as a stepfamily or blended family because that nomenclature feels right for them, you have the right to use the term that best describes your family. This my friend is entirely up to you.

CHAPTER 10 | **DEEP FACTS & TAKEAWAYS**

1. Every day, approximately 1300 new stepfamilies are formed.

2. Over fifty percent of US families are remarried or recoupled.

3. American marriages last an average of seven years.

4. Divorce occurs in one out of two marriages.

5. Approximately 75% of divorced couples remarry

6. When children are involved, 66% of couples living together or remarried will break up.

7. Approximately 80% of remarried, or re-coupled, partners with children have careers.

8. Over half of the 60 million children under the age of 13 live with one biological parent and that parent's current partner.

9. According to the 1990 US Census, there will be more stepfamilies by the year 2000 than original families.

10. According to research conducted by the Stepfamily Foundation, more than 60% of divorced fathers visit their children. However, these children do not legally reside with their fathers. Accordingly, neither government nor academic research includes these fathers and their children as stepfamilies. While the father may be a single parent, most likely he is re-married or re-

coupled, thus creating a stepfamily. Consequently, a large number of stepfamilies are formed as these children shuttle between their parents' homes. Many of these fathers go unnoticed and unaccounted for.

11. Seventy-five percent of stepfamilies report "not having access to resources as a stepfamily," according to a recent Stepfamily Foundation survey of 2000 online questionnaires.

12. Researchers at Boston University found that of the women who earned over $100,000 and had married men with children, over 75% stated that they would not marry a man with children if they had the opportunity to do it again.

13. According to research compiled by Professor of Sociology Larry L. Bumpass at the University of Wisconsin, about half of all women, not only mothers, will live in a stepfamily relationship at some point in their lives.

RELATIONSHIP IQ | **INSIGHTFUL QUESTIONS**

- Have you learned anything from your previous relationships that you wish to avoid in this one?

- Are you required to pay child support? In this case, how will they affect our financial situation, including any future children we may have together?

- Are we on the same page regarding finances? Will we have separate accounts or will we share one? Should we enter into a prenuptial agreement? Would you like me to contribute financially to your children?

- What should I do if your beautiful tween daughter is downright mean to me?
- Would you be open to my suggestions regarding the parenting of your children? Are there any restrictions?
- What expectations do you have about the relationship between me and your children? What will we do if they do not like me or I do not like them?
- Do you expect me to interact with your ex-partner? What is my role in co-parenting?
- How will you introduce me to your ex-partner? How will you introduce me to others when your ex is present?
- What is the attitude of your parents and extended family towards your ex-partner? How do you see my role in this situation?
- In the event that the ex fails to comply with the parenting arrangements, how will we deal with it as a couple?
- What will you do if your ex speaks negatively about me to you, the children, family members, or friends?
- What is our approach to conflict? How can we improve?
- Does each of us have a team of support around us? Alternatively, what can we do to support each other so that it becomes a reality?

- If we move in or get married, are there things we expect to change? Regarding each other? What about the children? What is the parenting arrangement?

- Is it my intention to love these children as if they were my own?

- Can I provide for these children as if they were my own?

- Is it my intention to put my family first?

- Is it my vow to love myself even when I am criticized?

- What will my spouse's role be in parenting the children if we are both parents?

- How confident am I that I will be able to add value and purpose to these kids and my partner, as well as myself?

- Is it okay that my beloved husband or wife must maintain a healthy relationship with his or her ex-spouse (or at least try to maintain that relationship)?

EPILOGUE

In my view, getting married is quite possibly one of the most significant undertakings one will ever experience in life. Next, of course, is having children. And then purchasing a home is also a big deal. In some respects, these three huge milestones that people experience in life are intertwined. This makes the information you have read in this book so valuable. Your future and your children's future depend on you to make strategic decisions regarding your life. If nothing else, I hope you exit this space that we have shared feeling more empowered, inspired, and determined to be more focused in your relationships and more mindful.

With that said, I want to congratulate you on your current or future engagement to the love of your lifetime. When most couples enter this phase of their union, it is not uncommon for either partner to envision their lives and the moments that they will share. Typically, couples never consider marriage counseling or premarital investigation during their relationship. When people determine to marry, premarital counseling or investigation is not a thought in mind or a topic of discussion. But it should be!

While there is no such thing as a perfect relationship, marriage counseling can steer both you and your partner toward an ideal direction for your union. You and your partner may benefit from therapy if you are experiencing issues that are common to married couples. Often, people think that therapists are only for those experiencing difficulties. However, therapy can help you and your spouse learns how to identify issues and handle conflicts that will likely arise in your relationship.

Ideally, a future husband and wife will be able to discuss conflict resolution strategies, such as making sure you are on the same page should an emergency occur, such as financial difficulties. This proactive strategy intends to prevent couples from engaging in negative behavior that often ends marriages, should those issues arise.

The following are some examples of topics that may be discussed during premarital counseling therapy sessions:

- Personal and joint finances
- Styles of parenting
- Methods of communication
- Conflict resolution techniques
- Types of decision-making
- Gender roles within a marriage
- Occupational therapy for families

In my view, most couples get married out of a sincere desire to be with one another. In essence, I do not believe that couples get married with the intentions, expectations, or desire of getting a divorce. Even so, I am not naive enough to think that couples do not get married knowing that a divorce is not an option. Before marrying again, my current wife and I agreed that divorce would not be an option for our relationship. In the past, both of us experienced failure in our relationships; therefore, we resolved that if we were ever to remarry, we would use what we learned about ourselves, our lives, our past experiences, and what we discovered during premarital counseling to create a relationship that would last.

When it comes to marriage, I would urge you to be sure of what you are getting into. I can assure you! It is not a decision that should be taken lightly. Marriage is not about fun and games. It is serious business. Partnership is at the heart of marriage. Partnering is about partnering for life and on everything with your potential spouse. Whether it is raising children, paying a mortgage, paying income taxes, or paying for a college education, marriage is a partnership. Due to the unique nature of this relationship, you must make decisions that are in accordance with the needs of the partnership. After marriage, it is no longer simply about you and what you require; it is also about the relationship as a whole. The importance of this element of marriage is often overlooked by people. In light of that understanding, it is critical to remember that marriage is not intended for selfish individuals.

Your marriage should be a partnership where you and your spouse can accomplish whatever is needed from the relationship. For this reason, you must know what you require as an individual. You cannot go into marriage in the discovery of yourself. You do that before you get married. This is a mistake that individuals often make. They get married with the hopes of finding themselves in the marriage. It would help if you did this before you got married. Ideally, marriage is about discovering each other and the possibilities of what your relationship and marriage can bring. I think some people enter marriage with a taste test philosophy. Essentially, they marry, intending to try it out, and if they do not like it, they end it and move on. This is what I experienced with the ending of my second marriage. As I look back on that blot in my life, she never intended to be with me for life. If I wasn't so broken and confused about life, I am confident that I would have not only recognized this reality. But I would not have involved myself in a relationship with her or anyone during this time, for I would have realized that a great deal of work was needed.

Couples often overlook the many benefits of working with a marriage and family therapist, including improving communication skills, and reducing conflict; it helps set the stage for both parties to seek professional assistance later in their relationship. During the premarital investigation phase, which includes counseling, these are things that you learn. Therapy is about peeling back the layers of who you are as a person and getting at the core of your humanity. This is the place where the basis of any relationship should be forged.

Many of the relationships experienced today are superficial. We started our journey together by saying that the last thing society needs to see is another couple that could not get the marriage thing right. Because of this reality, premarital counseling is a must.

Premarital Counseling

Marriage and family therapists provide premarital counseling, a specialized type of therapy that will benefit all couples contemplating a long-term commitment such as marriage. Premarital counseling teaches the couple how to handle conflict early on, before it becomes a severe problem, and communicate effectively before it escalates. Premarital counseling can also help partners better understand their expectations of marriage and resolve any significant differences in a neutral, safe environment.

Premarital Counseling Offers Many Benefits

Additionally, premarital counseling can assist couples in identifying areas that could lead to conflict in the future. While counseling offers immediate benefits and relationship solutions, it might also be able to help address future issues that may affect the well-being of the family. For instance, issues related to finances, child-rearing methods, and career goals should also be considered. Ideally, these issues should be resolved at the beginning of the relationship, but if it is not possible, develop a plan to address them later. According to a study published in the Journal of Family Psychology, couples who have participated in some premarital counseling programs are 31% less likely to divorce.

A healthy relationship can be founded through premarital counseling, couples' workshops, and other premarital services. According to research conducted by the institute, it takes six years for couples with problems to get professional help. Even couples with a relationship without any significant problems should get premarital counseling. Couples counseling is a good idea at the beginning of a long-term relationship because it allows each partner to express their thoughts, concerns, and expectations. It can help couples feel more at ease with therapy if they have problems in the future.

During premarital counseling sessions, couples can discuss finances, children, and intimacy. In my view, these are three major concerns for many couples. They can also develop communication skills and conflict resolution techniques and overcome fears about getting married, whether they stem from past relationship struggles or family background.

Premarital Counseling Providers

Marriage and family therapists often offer premarital counseling as part of their practice, which helps couples prepare for marriage or other long-term commitments. Counseling with a therapist, attending workshops or group therapy sessions, or participating in community programs are options available to couples seeking premarital counseling. If you don't want to go to therapy or can't get premarital counseling, you can easily access self-help books, DVDs, and other resources. Premarital counseling is required or strongly encouraged in some religions before marriage. A premarital counseling program is usually based on religion, with religious leaders acting as counselors, whether or not they are trained as therapists.

Premarital Counseling Challenges

Many couples delay or dread premarital counseling because they fear what may be revealed during the process. During counseling sessions, you can talk about complex topics or important things to yourself. It could be their first time talking about personal values and beliefs for some couples. Some couples might be able to address and resolve differences of opinion in therapy, but others could decide that certain things are irreconcilable and choose not to get married.

Therapists give participants a safe place to talk about concerns but hearing a partner talk about the relationship or their roles can be hurtful or lead to conflict. Couples can experience short-term conflict when discussing doubts, expectations, or goals about their relationship. Still, a lot of times, with the help of a therapist, they're able to work through it and build the foundation of a strong partnership.

Premarital counseling may not be available for every couple. It depends on the therapist. Some take insurance, and others don't. Counseling services may be available at local community centers and hospitals at a low cost. Your doctor or another health care professional can also tell you about low-cost counseling resources. In addition to being a time commitment, premarital counseling may be hard for busy couples to fit in. You can often talk to your therapist about flexible scheduling. If time and money are tight, premarital counseling can also be done using self-help books, DVDs, and audio.

Mental health professionals often contribute to these resources, which are not intended to take the place of professional counseling.

What To Expect From Premarital Counseling

Different therapists offer different premarital counseling. Depending on the therapist, they might work with each partner individually after a few sessions or work with them as a couple throughout therapy. The therapist can figure out what's bothering each partner, what they do well, and where they need improvement with these sessions. In the beginning, you might be able to speak openly and honestly about each other's goals for your partnership when you do it individually.

Additionally, each partner will be able to describe the ideal marriage they want for themselves, along with any steps they have taken to achieve it or any challenges they see standing in the way. Together, they can talk about these problems and, with a therapist's help, figure out how to handle them and any other issues that may come up throughout the marriage.

Counselors for couples help them develop something called a couple's resource map. This identifies resources to tap into when things get tough as a couple and individuals. As a couple, you can also discuss warning signs of trouble and devise a plan if these problems crop up. You can use this plan to seek support from individuals, talk to a counselor, or pray for guidance. By participating in premarital counseling, you will be able to initiate a partnership, such as marriage, that will benefit from counseling and improve and strengthen your relationship.

Discussing Important Issues

Premarital counseling gives you a chance to talk about several important things about your marriage, like:

- **Finances -** A couple's finances can be stressful and contentious, so you should decide how to handle your finances in advance.

- **Beliefs, Values, & Religion -** When you and your partner share your religious beliefs, values, and sentiments, it can help build better understanding and respect. Discussing the implications of these aspects in your daily life can also improve your relationship.

- **Roles in the Marriage -** You should discuss the roles you both expect to play in your wedding to prevent conflicts later.

- **Together Time & Activities -** You can talk about what you like doing together and how you plan to spend your time.

- **Children -** Many couples find they're not on the same page about having kids after marriage. Whether you want kids or not and how you want to raise them is something you need to decide in advance.

- **Family Relationships -** You might have concerns about your partner's family or your relationships with your family during premarital counseling.

Why Premarital Counseling Can Be Helpful

You and your partner can prepare for marriage by going through premarital counseling. Listed below are some things you can do with it.

- **Understanding Your Partner -** Premarital counseling can assist you in developing a deeper understanding of your spouse. It can help you better understand your partner's beliefs, motivations, priorities, values, expectations, and daily routine.

- **Setting Realistic Expectations -** A form of counseling lets you and your partner talk about all the essential things in marriage, so you know what to expect. As an individual and as a couple, it identifies your strengths and weaknesses.

- **Planning for the Future -** Just as you might consult with a wedding planner to plan your special day, a premarital counselor can assist you with planning your wedding and your life together.

Advantages of Premarital Counseling

You and your partner go to premarital counseling, so you know what to expect when you get married. Premarital counseling can help you deal with:

- **Communicate Constructively** - Premarital counseling emphasizes the importance of communication between partners, which means that partners are encouraged to convey their positions clearly without attacking or arming each other.

- **Develop Conflict Resolution Skills** - The purpose of marriage counseling is to help you and your partner deal with problems and resolve conflicts. Initially, communication can be a source of conflict, but couples can develop a constructive discussion with time.

- **Focusing on Positive Aspects** - Premarital counseling can help couples refocus their attention on the positive aspects of their relationship.

- **Eliminate Dysfunctional Behavior** - Premarital counseling can help identify unhealthy patterns and behaviors in a relationship.

- **Build Decision-Making Processes** - By participating in premarital counseling, you can establish an equitable and healthy decision-making process with your partner.

- **Alleviate Fears Related to Marriage** - Premarital counseling can be an excellent way for you or your partner to discuss critical issues and clarify what marriage will entail.

Getting premarital counseling lets you and your partner talk about and plan essential things about your marriage. You can get help from a counselor to make these conversations more productive. Furthermore, premarital counseling provides you with tools that make it easier to communicate and resolve conflicts.

With shows such as "Killer Relationship with Faith Jenkins?" Premarital Background checks should become standard practice, given the high divorce rate. Many people jump into a relationship without knowing who they're going to spend time with. Then they get married after a couple of months or years. They do not know about extravagant spending habits, past marriages, continuing affairs, etc. Getting a premarital background check is a great way to stay safe during the wedding. We don't want to marry someone who'll financially ruin us or our careers.

When it comes to marriage and divorce, there are four major issues. Money, infidelity, abuse, and personal values. What are your thoughts on all of these elements with your future spouse? Having money problems causes a ton of stress, so it's no surprise that money is a significant factor in divorces in the U.S. Divorces are caused by outstanding debts, spending habits, and unknown accounts. Money isn't the only thing that leads to divorce either. One of the reasons is that one spouse wants financial independence and secret accounts.

Even though it may sound unconventional, we live in a strange time. Have your spouse conduct a background check as well. A background check will include information about past financial obligations and responsibilities. The premarital report allows you and your spouse to lay down the cards and openly discuss the potential findings. You'll be able to share one more exciting thing with your future partner, and you'll know that if any of your secrets come out, so will theirs.

A person considering marriage wants to know that the person they will share their lives with is right for them. The most significant factor in finding the perfect spouse is love and emotions. Nevertheless, please don't ignore the fact that you can get impartial confirmation of what they say. You can get unbiased info from many sources, but a background check is one of the best. Besides, if your car lender or boss wants a background check, shouldn't a potential spouse also?

What can you learn from a background check if you're thinking of adding it to your relationship? Check out five common ones.

1. Criminal History

Every employer wants to make sure their employees don't have any criminal tendencies, and every spouse should want the same thing. Criminal background checks are standard background checks, and they can be reassuring. You can search many public court records with little effort, including arrest records, convicted crimes, and sentences.

2. Social Media Use

Today, social media gives you insight into someone's values, goals, and thoughts. The possibility of discovering older or less easily identifiable social media accounts that may shed new light on your loved one is possible if you follow their current social media accounts. An in-depth background check may even allow you to understand your loved one's relationships outside of your own.

Unlike many other records of an individual's life, social media links are publicly available without legal repercussions. It's also a great way to see your partner's personality through their friends and linked accounts.

3. Identity Checks

The issue of identity fraud isn't something most people think about, but it's getting worse. Identity issues can be found on two levels. You want to make sure the person you're going to marry is who they claim to be and that they don't hide anything from you. You also want to know if they have had any issues with identity theft since that could affect your relationship.

4. Marital Status

Have you and your future spouse previously been married? Have they got kids? Are you concerned about how your previous relationship ended? Marriage and divorce records are easy to call for a professional. It will save you time and frustration when you apply for your marriage license when you learn if your future spouse isn't legally divorced.

5. Financial Information

The financial responsibilities and the entanglements of marriage come with sharing life with a mate. It can take years or longer to work out these money problems, even if the marriage ends. As a result, you should find out as much as possible about their finances. Checking their credit history and state or federal tax status can help you determine if they've declared bankruptcy or are seriously delinquent. There can be a significant impact here, as things such as delinquent taxes will use up your funds. You can take precautions like avoiding mixing your finances when you know this.

As I look through the rearview mirror of my life, I should have waited until I was a mature adult before getting married, having sex, and making babies. As adults, in the wake of our bad decisions, the children suffer from not being reared in a loving home.

Over the years, I had learned to mask my ignorance about life with arrogance, and that mentality, coupled with a true gift for gab, allowed me to skate my way through life and a variety of different circumstances. I bought and believed in my hype throughout my teenage years, twenties, and thirties. Like most selfish people, I had a pretty inflated sense of self. In my world, how I saw it was how it was. I was right, and everyone else was wrong, and if their opinion didn't line up with mine, they were no longer welcome to offer me their opinion.

This was the case the day my Father told me that getting involved with my first wife wasn't a good idea and that I should focus my attention elsewhere. In similar fashion, this was also the case when my mother advised me to discard a credit card offer that arrived in the mail shortly before my 18th birthday. They both offered opinions that didn't align with what I wanted, so their views were discarded. My inability to listen to wisdom caused me to be in pretty bad shape financially, emotionally, and romantically.

Again, this is the compound effect of many errant unwise decisions. So, on the floor in my parent's den, I came clean with the Lord about everything that I found in me that was ugly. Why did I do this? I had reached a point where I decided I wanted to be free from my past. Moreover, I wanted to move forward. I realized that the only way I could do so was by accepting responsibility for my error and turning to the only source that could clean me up, give me perspective, and put me back on solid ground.

Acknowledging and Coping with Trauma

Friend, healing will not come from being dishonest about your past; healing comes from dealing with it for what it is and using what you've learned to catapult you positively into the next phase of your life. You must be honest with yourself. So, if your past relationship was based on sex, admit your mistake, and move on. If you got married too soon, acknowledge that it was too soon and move on. Listen, when it's all said and done, you are the only "YOU" that you have.

Based on all the information you have read in this self-help book, what have you learned about the importance of marriage? Likewise, what have you determined about your decision to get married?

- Does the person who considered getting married before reading this book still exist?

- Does the person you considered getting married to hold a flame in your eye still? Are they still the ones?

Listen, in life, as it may be in your choice to get married, it's important to remember that all things are not as simple as black and white. However, we can take solace in knowing that even when life presents us with shades of grey, if allowed, wisdom will take control and reveal a clear path, which will aid us in our effort to make choices based on fact than feeling. You see, my friend, it's in the soul where that combustible mix of human desire, raw emotion, burning flesh, lust, and temptation meet to form a cacophony of harsh, discordant sounds designed to rattle our thinking to hamper our ability to think.

If you have ever watched a professional golf tournament or football game, you may have seen a player or official motion to the crowd to bring the noise down. This action allows the players to focus on the moment's task to achieve the real purpose and goal of winning the game. If you are seriously considering getting married, one of the first things you must do is to take control of your emotions. It would help if you did a thoughtful review of yourself to understand that, as human beings, you and I are indeed nothing more than conflicted, complicated, confused, and often bewildered chess pieces played out on humanity's proverbial chessboard of good and evil.

The real problem that besets us all at one point or another is recognizing the path we're on and determining whether it's the right or wrong path. In this area, real wisdom is needed; it's where the real battles of life are won or lost—there are no ties or disqualifications. You either win the game, or you lose it. The battlefield of the mind and, indeed, for our minds began the day that you and I were created in the womb. A voice beckoned us to promise while another was beguiling us to trouble. So, it was in the beginning, and so it is today. You and I are tied in the now to a circumstance that happened ages ago.

It's because of a wrong decision, one of disobedience and, some might say, outright disregard for God's law, which we find ourselves today in one hell of a mess—running the race, crossing the finish line, and raising our hands in victory. Our race toward heaven's doors is every bit of a marathon and most certainly not a sprint. In this field of endurance, striving toward the most significant rewards are the pitfalls and dangers of life's uncertainties. The only assurance that each one of us has during this race is that he who endures until the end shall be saved. It is without question the dominant factor that motivates and encourages man through faith to pursue that which is righteous and brilliantly correct.

You have within your power the ability to make a choice. You can choose to follow the examples of men and women wise enough to make knowledge their ally or follow the fools that made folly their friend. You have the power to control your emotions and make decisions based on truths and facts. You can research, investigate, and evaluate all available proof to ensure that you're certain about the decisions you're inclined to make. It's up to you to decide based on the evidence presented and not the coercion or influence of man and his sinful tendencies. Your desire to join with someone in holy matrimony must be influenced by reasons carved from the foundational blocks of holiness.

Likewise, your decision to join in marriage should be a permanent position, not a temporary proposition. Although man has approved and made provisions for marital do-overs in the form of divorce, your race of endurance with your spouse should be based on the word of God and on the belief that marriage is a permanent situation, not a temporary solution. Thus, divorce is not an option. Your commitment to marriage should mirror your commitment to God. If you desire to do what is right by God's standards, you will carry this mindset into your marital relationship. However, suppose you are immoral as it relates to God, His context for life, marriage, and His express purpose for your existence.

In that case, your marriage will mirror your immoral lifestyle and behavior and eventually expose you as a fraud and your marriage to inevitable failure. Because you're reading this book, I have absolutely no doubt that making marriage work is your goal. But is that the goal of your potential spouse? If so, how do you know? Have you asked and received answers to those critical questions that require resolution before saying, "I DO!"? Have you examined the personal background of your potential spouse to determine whether there is a criminal history of some sort? Have you exchanged and examined each other's credit reports to see where you stand? Have you plowed your way past the idea of being married to get to the nuts and bolts of what marriage means and what it will mean for you?

You will experience hurt and pain that will challenge your resolve and perhaps even your very faith and belief in God in this lifetime. But some situations are simply self-inflicted and marrying a person without a complete understanding of what marriage is, what it does, what it means, and what it will mean for you is one of those circumstances.

Again, you have the power to make a choice. Perhaps in your research, investigation, and evaluation, you have honestly discovered or uncovered information that suggests the person you were considering marrying is not the right person for you. Don't be discouraged or feel pressured to ignore all empirical evidence because of age, finances, or other circumstances, and proceed with marriage anyway because it will be a disaster. A better way to approach this scenario is one of continued evaluation. It's possible that marriage to this person is not a good idea right now, but it doesn't necessarily mean you two can't be married in the future once those red flag conditions have been resolved. However, if through your examination you have determined that your potential spouse is not the right person for you, break it to them gently, explain your decision with humility, and move forward with your life.

If you must end the relationship, it's essential to do so positively. It will allow you both the closure you'll need to continue your journeys in life without the threads of hurt feelings that can extend into future relationships. However, suppose, after reading this book, you are fortunate enough to find that you and your potential significant other are indeed a match. In that case, I salute you and offer you my sincere and warmest congratulations. As you embark on your life journey together, remember that your union as man and woman is a unique union created by God. It would help if you kept your marital focus on the things in life that truly matter. If you do this, I know you'll have a love that shines like pure gold.

BIBLIOGRAPHY

1. Allemand M. Age differences in forgiveness: The role of future time perspective. *Journal of Research in Personality.* 2008;42:1137–1147. doi: 10.1037/a0031839. [CrossRef] [Google Scholar]

2. Barrett A. Marital trajectories and mental health. *Journal of Health and Social Behavior.* 2000;41:451–464. doi: 10.1007/s11205-007-9194-3. [PubMed] [CrossRef] [Google Scholar]

3. Beach SRH, Katz J, Kim S, Brody GH. Prospective effects of marital satisfaction on depressive symptoms in established marriages: A dyadic model. *Journal of Social and Personal Relationships.* 2003;20:355–371. doi: 10.1177/0265407503020003005. [CrossRef] [Google Scholar]

4. Bernard J. *The future of marriage.* New York: Bantam; 1972. [Google Scholar]

5. Bloch L, Haase CM, Levenson RW. Emotion regulation predicts marital satisfaction: more than a wives' tale. *Emotion.* 2014;14:130–144. doi: 10.1037/a0034272. [PMC free article] [PubMed] [CrossRef] [Google Scholar]

6. Boerner K, Jopp D, Carr D, Sosinsky L, Kim S-L. "His" and "her" marriage? Exploring the gendered facets of marital quality in later life. *Journals of Gerontology Series B: Psychological Sciences Social Sciences.* 2014;69 doi: 10.1093/geronb/gbu032579-589. [CrossRef] [Google Scholar]

7. Bookwala J. Marriage and other partnered relationships in middle and late adulthood. In: Blieszner R, Bedford VH, editors. *Handbook of aging and the family.* 2. Santa Barbara, CA: ABC-CLIO; 2012. pp. 91-124. [Google Scholar]

8. Broman CL. Marital quality in Black and White marriages. *Journal of Family Issues.* 2005;26:431-441. doi: 10.1177/0192513X04272439. [CrossRef] [Google Scholar]

9. Bulanda JR. Gender, marital power, and marital quality in later life. *Journal of Women & Aging.* 2011;23:2-22. doi: 10.1080/08952841.2011.540481. [PubMed] [CrossRef] [Google Scholar]

10. Butterworth P, Rodgers B. Concordance in the mental health of spouses: Analysis of a large national household panel survey. *Psychological Medicine.* 2006;36:685-697. doi: 10.1017/S003329170500667. [PubMed] [CrossRef] [Google Scholar]

11. C, Bento. Leal III. "4 Essential Keys to Effective Communication in Love, Life, Work-Anywhere!.", 1st ed., CreateSpace Independent Publishing Platform, 2017.

12. Carr D, Boerner K. Do spousal discrepancies in marital quality assessments affect psychological adjustment to widowhood? *Journal of Marriage and Family.* 2009;71:495-509. doi: 10.1111/j.1741-3737.2009.00615. [CrossRef] [Google Scholar]

13. Carr D, Boerner K, Moorman SM. End-of-life planning in a family context: Does relationship quality affect whether (and with whom) older adults plan? *Journals of Gerontology Series B: Psychological*

Sciences and Social Sciences. 2013;68:586–592. doi: 10.1093/geronb/gbt034. [PMC free article] [PubMed] [CrossRef] [Google Scholar]

14. Carr D, Springer KW. Advances in families and health research in the 21st century. *Journal of Marriage and Family.* 2010;72:743–761. doi: 10.1111/j.1741-3737.2010.00728. [CrossRef] [Google Scholar]

15. Carstensen L. Socioemotional selectivity theory: Social activity in life-span context. *Annual Review of Gerontology and Geriatrics.* 1991;11:195–217. [Google Scholar]

16. Chapman, Gary. "Building Love Together in Blended Families: The 5 Love Languages and Becoming Stepfamily Smart.", Moody Publishers, 2020.

17. Chapman, Gary. "The five Love Languages: The Secret to Love that Lasts.", Northfield Publishing, 1992.

18. Charles ST, Mather M, Carstensen LL. Aging and emotional memory: The forgettable nature of negative images for older adults. *Psychology and Aging.* 2003;23:495–504. doi: 10.1037/0096-3445.132.2.310. [PubMed] [CrossRef] [Google Scholar]

19. Cohen O, Geron Y, Farchi A. Marital quality and global well-being among older adult Israeli couples in enduring marriages. *The American Journal of Family Therapy.* 2009;37:299–317. doi: 10.1080/01926180802405968. [CrossRef] [Google Scholar]

20. Cook WL, Kenny DA. The actor–partner independence model: A model of bidirectional effects in developmental studies. *International Journal of Behavioral Development.* 2005;29:101–109. doi: 10.1080/0165025044400038. [CrossRef] [Google Scholar]

21. Davila J, Karney BR, Hall TW, Bradbury TN. Depressive symptoms and marital satisfaction: Within-subject associations and the moderating effects of gender and neuroticism. *Journal of Family*

Psychology. 2003;17:537–570. doi: 10.1037/0893-3200.17.4.557. [PubMed] [CrossRef] [Google Scholar]

22. Dehle C, Weiss RL. Sex differences in prospective associations between marital quality and depressed mood. *Journal of Marriage and the Family.* 1998;60:1002–1011. doi: 10.2307/353641. [CrossRef] [Google Scholar]

23. Diener E, Lucas RE, Scollon CN. Beyond the hedonic treadmill: Revising the adaptation theory of well-being. *American Psychologist.* 2006;61:305–314. doi: 10.1007/s10902-005-5683-8. [PubMed] [CrossRef] [Google Scholar]

24. Dockray S, Grant N, Stone AA, Kahneman D, Wardle J, Steptoe A. A comparison of affect ratings obtained with ecological momentary assessment and the Day Reconstruction Method. *Social Indicators Research.* 2010;99:269–283. doi: 10.1007/s11205-010-9578-7. [PMC free article] [PubMed] [CrossRef] [Google Scholar]

25. Dykstra PA, Gierveld J. Gender and marital history differences in emotional and social loneliness among Dutch older adults. *Canadian Journal on Aging.* 2004;23:141–155. doi: 10.1353/cja.2004.0018. [PubMed] [CrossRef] [Google Scholar]

26. Federal Interagency Forum on Aging-Related Statistics. *Older Americans 2012: Key indicators of well-being.* Washington, DC: U.S Government Printing Office; 2012. [Google Scholar]

27. Fincham FD, Beach SRH, Harold GT, Osborne LN. Marital satisfaction and depression: Different causal relationships for men and women? *Psychological Science.* 1997;8:351–357. doi: 10.1037/0022-3514.64.3.442. [CrossRef] [Google Scholar]

28. Finnas F, Nyqvist F, Saarela J. Some methodological remarks on self-rated health. *The Open Public Health Journal.* 2008;1:32–39. [Google Scholar]

29. Floure, Naideen. "The Basics: Understanding & Building Business Credit.", 2021.

30. Freedman VA, Cornman JC. *The Panel Study of Income Dynamics' Supplement on Disability and Use of Time (DUST) User Guide: Release 2009*. Vol. 1 Ann Arbor: Institute for Social Research, University of Michigan; 2012. [Google Scholar]

31. Frijters P, Beatton T. The mystery of the *U*-shaped relationship between happiness and age. *Journal of Economic Behavior & Organization*. 2012;82:525–42. doi: 10.1016/j.jebo.2012.03.008. [CrossRef] [Google Scholar]

32. Gaye, Jan and Ritz, David. "After the Dance: My Life with Marvin Gaye Hardcover.", Amistad Publishers, 2015.

33. George LK. Still happy after all these years: Research frontiers on subjective well-being in later life. *Journals of Gerontology Series B: Psychological Sciences and Social Sciences*. 2010;63B:331–339. doi: 10.1093/geronb/gbq006. [PubMed] [CrossRef] [Google Scholar]

34. Glenn ND, Weaver CN. The contribution of marital happiness to global happiness. *Journal of Marriage and the Family*. 1981;43:161–168. doi: 10.1086/268632. [CrossRef] [Google Scholar]

35. Hagedoorn M, van Yperen NW, Coyne JC, van Jaarsveld CHM, Ranchor AV, van Sonderen E, Sanderman R. Does marriage protect older people from distress? The role of equity and recency of bereavement. *Psychology and Aging*. 2006;21:611–620. doi: 10.1037/0882-7974.21.3.611. [PubMed] [CrossRef] [Google Scholar]

36. Heavey CL, Layne C, Christensen A. Gender and conflict structure in marital interaction: A replication and extension. *Journal of Consulting and Clinical Psychology*. 1993;61:16–27. doi: 10.1037/0022-006X.61.1.16. [PubMed] [CrossRef] [Google Scholar]

37. Hill MS. *The Panel Study of Income Dynamics: A user's guide*. Newbury Park, CA: Sage; 1992. [Google Scholar]

38. Holley SR, Haase CM, Levenson RW. Age-related changes in demand–withdraw communication behaviors. *Journal of Marriage and Family.* 2013;75:822-836. doi: 10.1111/jomf.12051. [PMC free article] [PubMed] [CrossRef] [Google Scholar]

39. Iida M, Shrout PE, Laurenceau J-P, Bolger N. Using diary methods in psychological research. In: Cooper H, Camic PM, Long DL, Panter AT, Rindskopf D, Sher KJ, editors. *APA handbook of research methods in psychology, Vol 1: Foundations, planning, measures, and psychometrics.* Washington, DC: American Psychological Association; 2012. pp. 277-305. [Google Scholar]

40. Iveniuk J, Waite LJ, Laumann E, McClintock MK, Tiedt AD. Marital conflict in older couples: Positivity, personality, and health. *Journal of Marriage and Family.* 2014;76:130-144. doi: 10.1111/jomf.1208. [PMC free article] [PubMed] [CrossRef] [Google Scholar]

41. Jackson JB, Miller RB, Oka M, Henry RG. Gender differences in marital satisfaction: A meta-analysis. *Journal of Marriage and Family.* 2014;76:105-129. doi: 10.1111/jomf.12077. [CrossRef] [Google Scholar]

42. James JB, Lewkowicz C, Libhaber J, Lachman M. Rethinking the gender identity crossover hypothesis: A test of a new model. *Sex Roles.* 1995;32:185-207. doi: 10.1007/BF01544788. [CrossRef] [Google Scholar]

43. Kahneman D, Krueger A, Schkade D, Schwarz N, Stone A. Would you be happier if you were richer? A focusing illusion. *Science.* 2006 Jun 30;312:1908-1910. doi: 10.1126/science.1129688. [PubMed] [CrossRef] [Google Scholar]

44. Kaufman G, Taniguchi H. Gender and marital happiness in later life. *Journal of Family Issues.* 2006;27:735-757. doi: 10.1177/0192513X05285293. [CrossRef] [Google Scholar]

45. Krause N. Race differences in life satisfaction among aged men and women. *Journals of Gerontology.* 1993;48:235-244. doi: 10.1093/geronj/48.5.S235. [PubMed] [CrossRef] [Google Scholar]

46. Krueger A, Schkade D. The reliability of subjective well-being measures. *Journal of Political Economics.* 2008;92:1833-1845. [PMC free article] [PubMed] [Google Scholar]

47. Kulik L. His and her marriage: Differences in spousal perceptions of marital life in late adulthood. In: Shohov SP, editor. *Advances in psychology research.* Huntington, NY: Nova Science; 2002. pp. 21-32. [Google Scholar]

48. Lang FR. Regulation of social relationships in later adulthood. *Journals of Gerontology Series B: Psychological Sciences and Social Sciences.* 2001;56B:321-326. doi: 10.1093/geronb/56.6.P321. [PubMed] [CrossRef] [Google Scholar]

49. Loscocco K, Walzer S. Gender and the culture of heterosexual marriage in the United States. *Journal of Family Theory & Review.* 2013;5:1-14. doi: 10.1111/jftr.12003. [CrossRef] [Google Scholar]

50. Luong G, Charles ST, Fingerman SL. Better with age: Social relationships across adulthood. *Journal of Social and Personal Relationships.* 2011;28:9-23. doi: 10.1177/0265407510391362. [PMC free article] [PubMed] [CrossRef] [Google Scholar]

51. Meyer, Joyce. "Approval Addiction: Overcoming Your Need to Please Everyone.", FaithWords publishing, 2005.

52. McGonagle K, Schoeni R. *The Panel Study of Income Dynamics: Overview and summary of scientific contributions after nearly 40 years. Technical Series Paper No 06-01.* 2006 Retrieved from http://psidonline.isr.umich.edu/Publications/Papers/tsp/2006-01_PSID_Overview_and_summary_40_years.pdf.

53. Mirecki RM, Chou JL, Elliott M, Schneider CM. What factors influence marital satisfaction? Differences between first and second

marriages. *Journal of Divorce & Remarriage.* 2013;54:78–93. doi: 10.1080/10502556.2012.743831. [CrossRef] [Google Scholar]

54. Mroczek DK, Spiro A. Change in life satisfaction during adulthood: Findings from the Veterans Affairs Normative Aging Study. *Journal of Personality and Social Psychology.* 2005;88:189–202. doi: 10.1037/0022-3514.88.1.189. [PubMed] [CrossRef] [Google Scholar]

55. Pinquart M, Sorensen S. Gender differences in caregiver stressors, social resources, and health: An updated meta-analysis. *Journals of Gerontology Series B: Psychological Sciences and Social Sciences.* 2006;61:33–45. [PubMed] [Google Scholar]

56. Proulx CM, Helms HM, Buehler C. Marital quality and personal well-being: A meta-analysis. *Journal of Marriage and Family.* 2007;69:576–593. doi: 10.1111/j.1741-3737.2007.00393.x. [CrossRef] [Google Scholar]

57. Quirouette C, Pushkar-Gold D. Spousal characteristics as predictors of well-being in older couples. *International Journal of Aging & Human Development.* 1992;34:257–269. [PubMed] [Google Scholar]

58. Revenson T, Kayser K, Bodenmann G, editors. *Emerging perspectives on couples' coping with stress.* Washington, DC: American Psychological Association; 2005. [Google Scholar]

59. Ryff CD, Singer B. The contours of positive human health. *Psychological Inquiry.* 1998;9:1–28. doi: 10.1207/s15327965pli0901_1. [CrossRef] [Google Scholar]

60. Schwarz N, Strack F. Reports of subjective well-being: Judgmental processes and their methodological implications. In: Kahneman D, Diener E, Schwarz N, editors. *Well-being: The foundations of hedonic psychology.* New York: Russell Sage Foundation; 1999. pp. 61–84. [Google Scholar]

61. Snyder, Stephen. "Credit After Bankruptcy: A Step-By-Step Action Plan to Quick and Lasting Recovery after Personal Bankruptcy.",2005.

62. Strack F. "Order effects" in survey research: Activation and information functions of preceding questions. In: Schwarz N, Sudman S, editors. *Contexts effects in social and psychological research*. New York: Springer-Verlag; 1992. [Google Scholar]

63. Teasdale JD, Taylor R, Fogarty SJ. Effects of induced elation: Depression on the accessibility of memories of happy and unhappy experiences. *Behaviour Research and Therapy*. 1980;18:339–346. [PubMed] [Google Scholar]

64. Tyndale. "The Holy Bible: New Living Translation.", Tyndale House Publishers, 1996.

65. The Holy Bible: King James Version.", Dallas, TX: Brown Books Publishing, 2004.

66. Umberson D, Pudrovska T, Reczek C. Parenthood, childlessness, and well-being: A life course perspective. *Journal of Marriage and Family*. 2010;72:621–629. doi: 10.1111/j.1741-3737.2010.00721.x. [PMC free article] [PubMed] [CrossRef] [Google Scholar]

67. Umberson D, Williams K, Powers DA, Liu H, Needham B. You make me sick: Marital quality and health over the life course. *Journal of Health and Social Behavior*. 2006;47:1–16. doi: 10.1177/002214650604700101. [PMC free article] [PubMed] [CrossRef] [Google Scholar]

68. Weathers R. *A guide to disability statistics from the American Community Survey*. Ithaca, NY: Employment and Disability Institute, Cornell University; 2005. [Google Scholar]

69. Whalen HR, Lachman ME. Social support and strain from partner, family and friends: Costs and benefits for men and women in adulthood. *Journal of Social and Personal Relationships*. 2000;17:5–30. doi: 10.1177/0265407500171001. [CrossRef] [Google Scholar]

70. Whisman MA. The association between depression and marital satisfaction. In: Beach SRH, editor. *Marital and family processes in depression: A scientific foundation for clinical practice.* Washington, DC: American Psychological Association; 2001. [Google Scholar]

71. Whisman MA, Uebelacker LA, Tolejko N, Chatav Y, Meckelvie M. Marital discord and well-being in older adults: Is the association confounded by personality? *Psychology and Aging.* 2006;21:626–631. doi: 10.1037/0882-7974.21.3.626. [PubMed] [CrossRef] [Google Scholar]

72. Whisman MA, Uebelacker LA, Weinstock LM. Psychopathology and marital satisfaction: The importance of evaluating both partners. *Journal of Consulting and Clinical Psychology.* 2004;72:830–838. doi: 10.1037/0022-006X.72.5.830. [PubMed] [CrossRef] [Google Scholar]

73. White L, Rogers SJ. Economic circumstances and family outcomes: A review of the 1990s. *Journal of Marriage and the Family.* 2000;62:1035–1051. doi: 10.1111/j.1741-3737.2000.01035.x. [CrossRef] [Google Scholar]

74. Williamson GM, Shaffer DR. Relationship quality and potentially harmful behaviors by spousal caregivers: How we were then, how we are now. *Psychology and Aging.* 2001;16:217–226. doi: 10.1037/0882-7974.16.2.217. [PubMed] [CrossRef] [Google Scholar]

75. Windsor TD, Ryan LH, Smith J. Individual well-being in middle and older adulthood: Do spousal beliefs matter? *Journals of Gerontology Series B: Psychological Sciences and Social Sciences.* 2009;64B:586–596. doi: 10.1093/geronb/gbp058. [PMC free article] [PubMed] [CrossRef] [Google Scholar]

APPENDIX

9 EFFECTIVE STEPS TO FINDING YOUR SOULMATE

Creating a meaningful relationship can be challenging, but the rewards of being with someone who can be your rock during difficult times are immeasurable. Love is the force that binds two people together, but finding the right partner who will support you no matter what takes time and consideration. Making the commitment to an intimate relationship is not something to take lightly. However, when you find a person who can be your best friend and partner for life, the reward is worth the effort. Love is a powerful force that brings both parties joy and happiness. To assist you in your search for a life partner, we have compiled a list of nine effective steps to find your soulmate.

Identify Your Purpose for a Relationship and Potential Partner

Understanding your needs and wants in a relationship is helpful before searching for a partner. Ask yourself what you are looking for in a partner and be critical of your own logical side while doing so.

Identify Your Potential Spousal Candidate

Choosing a partner from a large pool of people can be overwhelming, but commitment is crucial in a marriage. A wrong choice can lead to emotional distress and financial costs associated with divorce.

Gather & Research Information on Your Potential Spouse

Getting to know your potential spouse is vital before making commitments. Love and emotions play a significant role, but gathering independent and reliable information is essential. Be sure to ask the right questions to learn more about the person. Learning their values, goals, and interests is key to ensuring the right match. It is also imperative to have honest and open communication with your partner.

Make sure you are transparent about your expectations and feelings to ensure the relationship is healthy and fulfilling for both of you.

Think About Your Alternatives To The Spouse In Consideration

Making informed decisions requires being open-minded and considering alternative viewpoints. Listening to and understanding each other's feelings is essential in any relationship. Effective communication can help bridge the gap between two people and give them a better understanding of each other. It can also help strengthen and deepen love bonds.

Investigate and Weigh the Information Collected

Weighing the evidence is necessary after gathering information and considering past relationships. It is important to assess the potential benefits and risks of each alternative. Once a decision is made, it is important to evaluate the consequences of the decision. This will help ensure that the decision is sound and will lead to positive outcomes. Additionally, it is important to remain open to change if the initial decision does not yield the desired results.

Analyze the Compatibility of Potential Spouses

Effective communication, probing, and asking direct questions help analyze potential partners' compatibility. It is essential to consider your personality type and preferred communication style. It is also important to be open and honest when having these conversations. This way, you can better understand the other person and identify areas of potential conflict or misunderstanding. Finally, it is important to remember that communication is a two-way street and to be open to other people's ideas and opinions.

Select Your Determined Alternative to the Spouse Selected

After completing research, evaluating options, and anticipating prospects, it is time to decide and act. After deciding, it is important to communicate effectively. Taking the time to explain your reasoning and the pros and cons of the different options can help your partner appreciate the thought process and help them understand why the decision was made. This can help create and maintain a healthy relationship.

Decide on Your Candidate & Take Action

Take action as soon as you decide and prepare an action plan to achieve your goals. Have an open and honest conversation with your partner. Be willing to listen and be heard. Prioritize your relationship and make time to reconnect.

Evaluation of Candidate:
How to Choose Your Ideal Life Partner

Choosing the right life partner is one of the most critical decisions you will ever make. Finding a partner who is not only compatible but also trustworthy and supportive is essential to building a lasting, fulfilling relationship. This section will discuss how to evaluate a potential life partner and what characteristics to look for in a candidate.

Identifying Your Ideal Partner

Before jumping into a relationship, taking the time to evaluate the person you are interested in marrying is essential. The first step is to reflect on how you identified this person and whether they are a good match. Consider if they meet your requirements for a life partner and possess the qualities and values that are important to you. Evaluating a candidate takes time, and avoiding rushing into a commitment is essential.

Characteristics to Look For

When searching for a partner, it is important to keep an eye out for certain characteristics that can make or break a relationship. Here are six key traits to look for in a potential partner:

1. **Communication Skills:** Good communication is the foundation of a strong relationship. You want someone you can easily communicate with and be open to discussing different topics and activities.

2. **Shared Interests:** While having identical interests is unnecessary, finding someone with whom you share

common hobbies or passions can make your time together more enjoyable and fulfilling.

3. **Compatibility:** Think about your partner's intelligence and personality traits. While differences can be exciting, finding someone who complements your strengths and weaknesses is important.

4. **Standards:** While respecting differences is important, having standards for what you want in a partner is essential. Do not compromise on important qualities, such as respect, kindness, and honesty.

5. **Trustworthiness:** Trust and belief are crucial to a happy marriage. Look for someone who is dependable, honest, and willing to be vulnerable with you.

6. **Time Together:** Spending quality time together is essential for building a strong relationship. Look for a partner who values your time and tries to prioritize your relationship.

Final Thoughts

Choosing the right life partner requires time, patience, and careful consideration. Remember to reflect on your needs and values and watch for someone who complements and supports them. Communication, shared interests, compatibility, standards, trustworthiness, and time together are all important characteristics to look for in a potential partner. By evaluating candidates thoughtfully and honestly, you will increase your chances of finding the right person for you.

VERSES FROM THE BIBLE RELATED TO LOVE, HONOR & COMMITMENT

Hebrews 13:4 ~ Let marriage be held in honor among all, and let the marriage bed be undefiled, for God will judge the sexually immoral and adulterous.

Proverbs 18:22 ~ He who finds a wife finds a good thing and obtains favor from the Lord.

Genesis 2:24 ~ Therefore a man shall leave his father and his mother and hold fast to his wife, and they shall become one flesh.

1 Corinthians 13:4-7 ~ Love is patient and kind; love does not envy or boast; it is not arrogant or rude. It does not insist on its own way; it is not irritable or resentful; it does not rejoice at wrongdoing but rejoices with the truth. Love bears all things, believes all things, hopes all things, endures all things.

John 14:27 ~ Peace I leave with you; my peace I give you. I do not give to you as the world gives. Do not let your hearts be troubled and do not be afraid.

Proverbs 21:9 ~ It is better to live in a corner of the housetop than in a house shared with a quarrelsome wife.

Proverbs 19:14 - House and wealth are inherited from fathers, but a prudent wife is from the Lord.

1 Peter 3:7 ~ Likewise, husbands, live with your wives in an understanding way, showing honor to the woman as the weaker vessel, since they are heirs with you of the grace of life, so that your prayers may not be hindered.

2 Corinthians 6:14 ~ Do not be unequally yoked with unbelievers. For what partnership has righteousness with lawlessness? Or what fellowship has light with darkness?

1 Peter 4:8 ~ Above all, keep loving one another earnestly, since love covers a multitude of sins.

Colossians 3:14 ~ And above all these put on love, which binds everything together in perfect harmony.

John 13:34-35 ~ A new commandment I give to you, that you love one another: just as I have loved you, you also are to love one another. By this all people will know that you are my disciples, if you have love for one another."

John 15:13 ~ Greater love has no one than this, that someone lay down his life for his friends.

1 Corinthians 13:13 ~ So now faith, hope, and love abide, these three; but the greatest of these is love.

1 Corinthians 13:4-8 ~ Love is patient and kind; love does not envy or boast; it is not arrogant or rude. It does not insist on its own way; it is not irritable or resentful; it does not rejoice at wrongdoing but rejoices with the truth. Love bears all things, believes all things, hopes all things, endures all things. Love never ends. As for prophecies, they will pass away; as for tongues, they will cease; as for knowledge, it will pass away.

1 Corinthians 16:14 ~ Let all that you do be done in love.

John 3:16 ~ "For God so loved the world, that he gave his only Son, that whoever believes in him should not perish but have eternal life.

1 John 4:7-8 ~ Beloved, let us love one another, for love is from God, and whoever loves has been born of God and knows God. Anyone who does not love does not know God, because God is love.

Ephesians 5:25 ~ Husbands, love your wives, as Christ loved the church and gave himself up for her

Ephesians 5:25 ~ Husbands, love your wives, as Christ loved the church and gave himself up for her

Ephesians 5:33 ~ However, let each one of you love his wife as himself, and let the wife see that she respects her husband.

Genesis 2:18 ~ Then the Lord God said, "It is not good that the man should be alone; I will make him a helper fit for him."

Matthew 19:4-6 ~ He answered, "Have you not read that he who created them from the beginning made them male and female, and said, 'Therefore a man shall leave his father and his mother and hold fast to his wife, and the two shall become one flesh'? So they are no longer two but one flesh. What therefore God has joined together, let not man separate."

Colossians 3:18-19 ~ Wives, submit to your husbands, as is fitting in the Lord. Husbands, love your wives, and do not be harsh with them.

1 Peter 4:8 ~ Above all, keep loving one another earnestly, since love covers a multitude of sins.

Proverbs 31:10 ~ An excellent wife who can find? She is far more precious than jewels.

Mark 10:6-9 ~ But from the beginning of creation, 'God made them male and female.' 'Therefore a man shall leave his father and mother and hold fast to his wife, and the two shall become one flesh.' So they are no longer two but one flesh. What therefore God has joined together, let not man separate."

Romans 8:28 ~ And we know that in all things God works for the good of those who love him, who have been called according to his purpose.

Ephesians 5:22-33 ~ Wives, submit yourselves to your own husbands as you do to the Lord. For the husband is the head of the wife as Christ is the head of the church, his body, of which he is the Savior. Now as the church submits to Christ, so also wives should submit to their husbands in everything. Husbands, love your wives, just as Christ loved the church and gave himself up for her to make her holy, cleansing her by the washing with water through the word, and to present her to himself as a radiant church, without stain or wrinkle or any other blemish, but holy and blameless. In this same way, husbands ought to love their wives as their own bodies. He who loves his wife loves himself. After all, no one ever hated their own body, but they feed and care for their body, just as Christ does the church— for we are members of his body. "For this reason a man will leave his father and mother and be united to his wife, and the two will become one flesh." This is a profound mystery—but I am talking about Christ and the church. However, each one of you also must love his wife as he loves himself, and the wife must respect her husband.

1 Corinthians 7:2-11 ~ But since sexual immorality is occurring, each man should have sexual relations with his own wife, and each woman with her own husband. The husband should fulfill his marital duty to his wife, and likewise the wife to her husband. The wife does not have authority over her own body but yields it to her husband. In the same way, the husband does not have authority over his own body but yields it to his wife. Do not deprive each other except perhaps by mutual consent and for a time, so that you may devote yourselves to prayer. Then come together again so that Satan will not tempt you because of your lack of self-control. I say this as a concession, not as a command. I wish that all of you were as I am. But each of you has your own gift from God; one has this gift, another has that. Now to the unmarried and the widows I say: It is good for them to stay unmarried, as I do. But if they cannot control themselves, they should marry, for it is better to marry than to burn with passion. To the married I give this command (not I, but the Lord): A wife must not separate from her husband. But if she does, she must remain unmarried or else be reconciled to her husband. And a husband must not divorce his wife.

Isaiah 62:5 ~ For as a young man marries a young woman, so shall your sons marry you, and as the bridegroom rejoices over the bride, so shall your God rejoice over you.

Deuteronomy 24:5 ~ When a man is newly married, he shall not go out with the army or be liable for any other public duty. He shall be free at home one year to be happy with his wife whom he has taken.

Ecclesiastes 4:12 ~ And though a man might prevail against one who is alone, two will withstand him—a threefold cord is not quickly broken.

Proverbs 12:4 ~ An excellent wife is the crown of her husband, but she who brings shame is like rottenness in his bones.

Ephesians 5:31 ~ "Therefore a man shall leave his father and mother and hold fast to his wife, and the two shall become one flesh."

1 Corinthians 16:13 ~ Be on your guard; stand firm in the faith; be courageous; be strong.

1 John 4:7 ~ Beloved, let us love one another, for love is from God, and whoever loves has been born of God and knows God.

Matthew 19:9 ~ And I say to you: whoever divorces his wife, except for sexual immorality, and marries another, commits adultery."

Matthew 5:32 ~ But I say to you that everyone who divorces his wife, except on the ground of sexual immorality, makes her commit adultery, and whoever marries a divorced woman commits adultery.

Ecclesiastes 4:9-12 ~ Two are better than one, because they have a good reward for their toil. For if they fall, one will lift up his fellow. But woe to him who is alone when he falls and has not another to lift him up! Again, if two lie together, they keep warm, but how can one keep warm alone? And though a man might prevail against one who is alone, two will withstand him—a threefold cord is not quickly broken.

Mark 10:9 ~ What therefore God has joined together, let not man separate.

Psalm 85:10 ~ Steadfast love and faithfulness meet; righteousness and peace kiss each other.

QUESTIONS YOU SHOULD ASK TO GAIN A DEEPER UNDERSTANDING OF YOUR PARTNER

Before Marriage

In order to obtain a deeper understanding of one another, you should ask some questions in addition to those you asked when you first started dating. It is advisable to ask these kinds of questions if a long-term relationship is to lead to marriage.

- ☐ Are you interested in having children?
- ☐ Do you like big or small families?
- ☐ What do you think about religion and spirituality?
- ☐ What's your dream place to live when you're older?
- ☐ Are you happy with your current job, or are you looking to switch?
- ☐ What's it like to be faithful to someone?

- ☐ What do you think of our sex life?

- ☐ Are you experiencing any financial difficulties?

- ☐ What is your drinking frequency?

- ☐ What made you decide to get married?

- ☐ What do you think of having one parent stay home with the kids, or do you think daycare (or a nanny) would be better?

- ☐ What would you consider the secret to a happy, long marriage (every couple has a few difficult moments!)?

- ☐ Do you have a favorite love language? Do you feel loved by someone you are in a relationship with? How do you express your love?

- ☐ Can you cope with difficult circumstances (e.g., grief, job loss, family stress, insufficient sleep, periods of overwhelming responsibility)?

- ☐ Are there any issues from your past that may become a problem in the future?

Marriage and Children

These are some questions you should ask your fiancé before you get married:

- ☐ What's the number of kids you want?

- ☐ How do you plan to install values in your children?

- ☐ What is your preferred method of disciplining your children?

- ☐ Are you concerned about what your child would do if he came out as homosexual?
- ☐ How would we feel if our children did not wish to attend college?
- ☐ What is the significance of children's voices in a family?
- ☐ What's your comfort level around kids?
- ☐ Would you mind if our parents watched the kids so we could hang out alone?
- ☐ What do you think about private vs. public schools?
- ☐ What do you think about homeschooling?
- ☐ Are you ok with adopting if we can't have kids?
- ☐ Would you consider seeking medical aid if we could not have children naturally?
- ☐ What do you think about disciplining your kid in public?
- ☐ Would you be willing to pay for your child's college education?
- ☐ What's the distance between you and your kids?
- ☐ Would you prefer someone to keep the kids at home or go to daycare?
- ☐ What if our kids decided to join the military instead of college?
- ☐ What's your idea of grandparent involvement?
- ☐ What's our plan for parent decisions?

Dealing With Conflict

You can make sure your relationship is healthy by answering these pre-marriage questions.

- ☐ What do you think about marriage counseling if we have problems?
- ☐ Where do you stand if I disagree with your family?
- ☐ What's your strategy for handling disagreements?
- ☐ Are you considering divorce?
- ☐ Would you rather talk when things come up or wait until things are bad?
- ☐ If you're not satisfied sexually, how would you say it?
- ☐ How should a couple resolve disagreements in their marriage?
- ☐ How can I communicate with you better?

Beliefs, Morals, Political Opinions, Religious Beliefs, & Family Values

Before you get serious about marriage, you should ask your fiancé these questions:

- ☐ How do you feel about infidelity?
- ☐ What's your religion's take on marriage?
- ☐ Whose priority is greater, work or family?
- ☐ How do you feel about politics?
- ☐ Can you tell me what you think about birth control?

- [ ] What would you rather have: a rich and miserable life or a poor and happy one?
- [ ] Who's going to make the most important decisions in the family?
- [ ] How would you handle someone saying bad things about you?
- [ ] Do you consider your family's advice more valuable than your spouse's?
- [ ] What's your ideal behavior for a wife?
- [ ] What are the responsibilities of household chores?
- [ ] What do you think a husband's role should be?

Handling Finances

Debt, finances, and money are important topics to discuss before getting married.

- [ ] What do you think about debt?
- [ ] How would you feel if the money was split between your spouse and you?
- [ ] What do you think about saving money?
- [ ] Can you tell me what you think about spending money?
- [ ] What if we are both interested in something, but we are both unable to afford it?
- [ ] Do you have a good budget?
- [ ] How important is it to save for retirement?

- ☐ How about getting a second job if we ran into financial problems?
- ☐ What are your debts?
- ☐ What if you want to borrow a lot of money from a family member?
- ☐ Who handles the household's finances?

Entertainment

Remember to enjoy yourself. Make sure your list of 100 questions for couples includes entertainment and lifestyle.

- ☐ Are you a fan of traveling?
- ☐ What is your preferred frequency of travel?
- ☐ What's your dream vacation?
- ☐ What's the importance of spending time alone for you?
- ☐ If I went on a trip with the girls (boys) for a few weeks, how would you feel?
- ☐ What's the importance of spending time with your friends?
- ☐ Can you tell me what you would like to do on a weekday evening?
- ☐ How would we spend our time if we both had the same weekend off from work? However, we had different plans for how to spend it?

Extended Family

Ask your partner some family and relationship questions among your 100 questions.

- ☐ What's your ideal frequency of visiting your family?
- ☐ How often are you going to visit us?
- ☐ What's the best time for my family to visit?
- ☐ How often do you want to visit my family?
- ☐ Are there any diseases or genetic abnormalities in your family history?
- ☐ How would you react if one of your family members disliked you?
- ☐ What would you do if your family visited over the holidays?
- ☐ Would you let your parents stay with you if they got sick?
- ☐ If my parents got sick, could you take them in?

Medical Information

Get to know your future husband or wife's family and medical history.

- ☐ Do you know anyone in your family who's an alcoholic?
- ☐ What is the medical history of your family?
- ☐ How would you feel about mental health treatment?
- ☐ Do you mind if I change my diet because of medical reasons?

- ☐ Is it possible that we can exercise together to improve our health?
- ☐ What's your dream place to live?
- ☐ Are you okay with me moving if I have to relocate for my job?

About the Relationship and Marriage

A list of 100 topics to discuss might seem excessive, but you can learn a great deal from 100 questions – for example, how your future spouse views marriage and relationships.

- ☐ If we were to break up, what would you do?
- ☐ Where do you see your career going?
- ☐ Where do you see yourself in five or ten years?
- ☐ How would you describe the best strategy to maintain love within a marriage?
- ☐ What would be the impact of our marriage on your life?
- ☐ What do you like about marriage?
- ☐ How do you describe the worst part of marriage?
- ☐ How would you spend the perfect weekend?
- ☐ What's the biggest thing for you about wedding anniversaries?
- ☐ What's your idea of a good time?
- ☐ How about becoming a grandparent someday?
- ☐ How do you envision your dream house?

- ☐ Do you have a marriage fear?
- ☐ How does the prospect of getting married excite you?
- ☐ Why are wedding rings important to you?
- ☐ How do you feel about talking to me about anything?
- ☐ Would you like us to have a better relationship?
- ☐ How would you change one aspect of our relationship?
- ☐ Is there anything you doubt about our future together?
- ☐ Do you believe that love can lift you out of any situation?
- ☐ Is there anything about me you are not confident of?
- ☐ What would you prefer - doing the dishes or doing the laundry?
- ☐ What's your favorite pet?
- ☐ How many pets are you interested in?
- ☐ What would you like to do with your retirement?
- ☐ Do you want to retire when you're a certain age?

General questions about attraction to ask your partner

There are times when you wish to learn about something despite the fact that the information cannot be categorized. Here you can find out the preferences of your partner, their way of conversing with others, and maybe even their wishes.

- ☐ How did you notice me first?
- ☐ Do you think physical attraction plays a role in getting into a relationship?

☐ How do you like women's scents?

☐ How would you describe your type? Are you looking for someone like me?

☐ What would you say about me to someone else?

☐ Do you have any tips for describing yourself to others?

☐ Would you like me to do anything else for you?

☐ What do you think the moment you see me?

☐ Why do you like me so much?

☐ What is your perspective on other men (women)?

☐ What three wishes would you like me to grant you?

☐ What are your goals for us?

☐ How did you feel when you first met me?

☐ How would you feel if my appearance changed drastically overnight (such as a new haircut or change in hair color) or over time (such as the addition of muscle and the loss of weight)?

☐ Can you give me an example of something you believe about me that you have never confirmed?

☐ What's the big deal for you regarding special occasions?

Relationship History

Before moving forward with a potential partner, some people want to know about their past. If you're considering marriage, feel free to ask anything you need to know. By asking these questions, you will have the opportunity to discover more about your partner's past.

- ☐ Do you have any experience with cheating on a partner? Even if you don't, are you thinking about it?
- ☐ How many ex-girlfriends or boyfriends have you had?
- ☐ How did you feel about asking me out? How did you decide against asking me out?
- ☐ What did you think when we first met?
- ☐ When was the last time you fell in love?
- ☐ Where did you get your role model from? Do you have any role models in your romantic life?
- ☐ What was it like when you finally realized you loved me?
- ☐ Would we have run into each other again if we hadn't dated and lost touch as we did?
- ☐ How did you discover me? What were you looking for? Would you consider yourself to be looking for love at all?

Relationship Future

Have you ever wondered if you and your partner are compatible? Consider your options carefully. Think about retirement planning as far in advance as you feel comfortable. However, be sure to weigh the span of time you have been together and the details that have already been talked about before asking. It is essential for you not to convey an improper message.

- ☐ What are your plans for this relationship in the coming year? How do you envision the relationship in five years?

- ☐ How do you feel about marriage and kids?

- ☐ What would you do if you found out I couldn't have children?

- ☐ What is your professional objective, and how might it affect our relationship?

- ☐ When you retire, where do you want to live?

- ☐ You deserve a good lover, and I'm here for you. Is there anything I can do to make you one?

- ☐ What would a day in a married couple's life with children look like? Would a week be any different?

- ☐ What do you think about providing our elderly parents with care if they cannot live independently one day?

- ☐ What is your plan for saving for retirement? Are there any specific goals?

Thoughts Involving Love

There are many ways to show your love, so it is important that you know what will make your partner pleased. You are probably interested in learning what your potential mate thinks and feels about love.

- ☐ How can I express my love for you?

- ☐ What do you think about soul mates? Do you believe in first love?

☐ In the past, did you ever feel hurt and question whether or not love is possible?

☐ What's the first time you realized you loved me?

☐ Were you hoping for a long-lasting relationship? Ever had any doubts?

☐ Which would you prefer: receiving a gift or having someone help you out?

☐ What's your favorite type of gift: a sentimental or practical one?

☐ What's your favorite way to express love?

☐ What kinds of compliments do you enjoy receiving?

Thoughts Involving Intimacy

The importance of intimacy in a serious relationship cannot be overstated. Intimacy extends beyond the bedroom. There is no way to avoid intimacy completely in a relationship. What you can do is plan dates based on your partner's preferences. This is perfectly normal. Take the time to ask questions and develop a relationship with your partner.

☐ What do you think about our relationship? Is there anything we can do to make it better?

☐ Would you like to be touched in a certain way and in a specific place?

☐ How would you like your fantasies to be fulfilled?

☐ Can you tell me what you think about toys?

☐ Would you like to try something we haven't tried?

☐ How often would you like to be intimate with me in the ideal situation (and in the real one)?

☐ How can I keep the intimacy going even if we're not together?

Text Questions

As texting has become the preferred method of communication for many couples, it should come as no surprise that intimate conversations can happen through text messages. If you feel embarrassed discussing intimate topics face to face, you might feel more comfortable asking intimate questions via text. Here are some questions you may find useful.

1. When you think of me, what is the thing you miss most?

2. Have you ever wanted to say something to me but weren't able to?

3. What do you want me to do when we're together next?

4. What would be the best place for me to kiss you?

5. Where have you ever felt closest to me?

6. Could you pick one word to describe our relationship?

7. Could you tell me how I could be a better partner?

An open-ended question can lead to a deep discussion and a deeper understanding between partners. These questions are designed to spark discussions about a person's true nature, which will then reveal the real you.

Revealing Questions

As a starting point for a more in-depth discussion, they can reveal more about your partner's personality and perspective on life.

- ☐ What do you admire most about them?
- ☐ Was your childhood enjoyable?
- ☐ How would you spend a million dollars if you had it to give away?
- ☐ What's your opinion on whether men and women are equal?
- ☐ Which is your greatest fear?
- ☐ Why do you get angry?
- ☐ If you were to describe your ideal life, what would it be?
- ☐ What do you think? Is there a stronger influence on people from their environment or their genes?
- ☐ How would you describe your purpose?
- ☐ Which person in your life is the villain?
- ☐ When people think of you, what do they say?
- ☐ When people talk about you, what do you want them to say?
- ☐ Do you have any things you would change about yourself?
- ☐ When was the last time you cried?

- ☐ Are you happy with what you've become now, or would Younger You be?
- ☐ Can you tell me what the best way for me to be your partner is?
- ☐ When it comes to your life, what's your most outstanding achievement?
- ☐ What's the most fantastic thing that's happened to you?
- ☐ Would you say or do anything that would make you less interested in spending time with me?
- ☐ What would you like to remember you for?
- ☐ Is there a way to express my appreciation and honor for you?
- ☐ Are there any things we can do to improve our relationship?
- ☐ How much do you think fate has to do with our lives?
- ☐ What makes you feel loved the most?
- ☐ Which part of your life would surprise me the most if I lived it for a day?
- ☐ Do you remember the last time your heart was broken?
- ☐ What do you think makes a relationship successful?
- ☐ Did you have a bad relationship in the past?
- ☐ Are you still in touch with your ex-boyfriends or ex-girlfriends?

- [ ] What have you done that you're most proud of?
- [ ] How did you feel about me when you first saw me?
- [ ] If you were a fantasy character, what would it be?
- [ ] If you had to choose one fear, what would it be?
- [ ] What do you wish you could change about yourself?
- [ ] If other people knew how you do it, there's probably something they'd consider weird.
- [ ] Is there something you regret doing (or not doing)?
- [ ] You could go on a date with any celebrity you wanted. Who would you choose and why?
- [ ] Did your parents have a good relationship?
- [ ] How were your relationships with your siblings?

RELATIONSHIP BLUEPRINT FOR BUILDING STRONG & HEALTHY CONNECTIONS

In this section, I will help you understand the importance of building safe, wholesome, and loving relationships. There is no doubt that relationships play a significant role in human behavior, shaping our society and communities. Positive relationships offer us a sense of security, support, and happiness that can help us overcome life's challenges.

Building a strong and healthy relationship can have a positive impact on your mental and physical health. When you have a supportive partner, you are more likely to experience a decrease in stress, anxiety, and depression. The mutual trust and respect that you have with your partner can provide a sense of emotional stability, leading to a more fulfilling life.

Solid relationships are essential for building healthy and productive communities. When people have supportive partners and families, they are more likely to feel connected to their community and to contribute positively to society. In contrast, broken relationships can lead to social isolation, substance abuse, and other negative outcomes.

It is important to ensure that you are compatible with the right people. If you are not careful, you could end up in a toxic and abusive relationship. The consequences of not picking the right partner can be devastating. Spouses who were abused, harmed, or even murdered by their partners, are tragic examples of what can happen when we ignore the warning signs.

Investigating the background of people, we are considering for long-term relationships or marriage is essential. We must identify red flags while dating to avoid becoming a victim of abuse or harm. My book provides a premarital investigations checklist that will help you identify potential issues before making a commitment. You will also find the steps for performing research and investigation of someone's background, providing you with the information you need to make an informed decision.

Properly evaluating the details, you have uncovered during the investigation is also critical. This section will provide you with the tools you need to make a determination to move forward with this person or to move on with your life. You deserve to be in a safe and loving relationship, and this book will help you achieve that goal.

Lastly, this section offers valuable insights into building healthy and safe relationships. You will find a checklist of 80 of the most critical red flags to consider when meeting a person, dating, considering a relationship, marriage, or having a child. Use these tools to ensure that you are building a fulfilling and lasting relationship that will bring joy and happiness into your life.

Premarital Investigation's Checklist

- ☐ **Criminal history:** Check if the person has any criminal record, especially for violent or abusive behavior, or a history of substance abuse.

- ☐ **Financial history:** Check if the person has any outstanding debt, bankruptcies, or financial obligations that could impact your future together.

- ☐ **Relationship history:** Investigate if the person has a history of unhealthy or abusive relationships, infidelity, or commitment issues.

- ☐ **Family background:** Look into the person's family background, including any history of mental illness, addiction, or abusive behavior.

- ☐ **Employment history:** Verify the person's employment history, including their current job status and stability.

- ☐ **Education and qualifications:** Confirm the person's education level and any professional qualifications they claim to have.

- ☐ **Personal values and beliefs:** Explore the person's personal values, beliefs, and attitudes towards religion, family, politics, and social issues.

- ☐ **Communication style:** Observe the person's communication style, including how they express themselves, listen to others, and resolve conflicts.

- ☐ **Interpersonal skills:** Evaluate the person's interpersonal skills, such as their ability to form and maintain healthy relationships, manage emotions, and handle stress.

- ☐ **Compatibility:** Assess the level of compatibility between you and the person in terms of goals, interests, lifestyle, and future plans.

- ☐ **Medical history:** Check if the person has any chronic illnesses, genetic conditions, or history of mental health issues.

- ☐ **Substance use:** Investigate if the person has a history of substance abuse, including alcohol, drugs, or prescription medication.

- ☐ **Legal issues:** Check if the person has any ongoing legal issues, such as lawsuits, custody battles, or immigration problems.

- ☐ **Social media:** Check the person's social media profiles for any red flags, such as offensive or inappropriate posts, or evidence of a double life.

□ **Friends and family:** Observe how the person interacts with their friends and family, and investigate if any of their close relationships could potentially be problematic.

□ **Travel history:** Check if the person has traveled extensively or lived abroad, as this may impact their views and attitudes towards life and relationships.

□ **Hobbies and interests:** Explore the person's hobbies and interests and consider if they align with yours and if they could potentially cause conflicts in the future.

□ **Emotional intelligence:** Assess the person's emotional intelligence, including their self-awareness, empathy, and ability to regulate emotions.

□ **Conflict resolution:** Observe how the person handles conflicts, including their communication style, willingness to compromise, and ability to forgive.

□ **Trustworthiness:** Evaluate the person's level of trustworthiness, including their honesty, integrity, and ability to keep promises.

Steps to Performing Research of A Person's Background

er basic information: Collect any basic
n that you have about the person, such
ame, date of birth, and current or previous
s.

2. **Conduct online research:** Use online resources such as search engines, social media, public records, and professional networking sites to gather more information about the person's background, including employment history, education, criminal record, and social activities.

3. **Interview references:** Contact references provided by the person or identified through research to verify information and gather additional details about the person's background.

4. **Verify information:** Verify any information gathered through research or interviews to ensure accuracy and reliability.

5. **Consider privacy and legal concerns:** Be mindful of privacy and legal concerns, such as obtaining consent for background checks, protecting confidential information, and avoiding discrimination.

6. **Document findings:** Document the findings of the investigation in a clear and organized manner, including any supporting evidence or documentation.

7. **Use information ethically:** Use the information gathered in an ethical and lawful manner, and avoid using it for purposes other than those intended by the investigation.

Steps to Performing An Investigation

1. **Define the problem:** Clearly define the problem or issue that needs investigation and establish the scope of the investigation.

2. **Plan the investigation:** Develop a plan for the investigation, including the methods to be used, the resources needed, and the timeline.

3. **Gather information:** Collect and gather information relevant to the investigation, including any documents, data, or physical evidence.

4. **Interview witnesses and subjects:** Conduct interviews with witnesses and any relevant subjects involved in the investigation and gather their statements and testimony.

5. **Analyze the information:** Review and analyze the information gathered to identify any patterns, inconsistencies, or relevant details.

6. **Draw conclusions:** Based on the information gathered and analyzed, draw conclusions about the issue or problem being investigated.

cument findings: Document the findings of the ation in a clear and organized manner, supporting evidence or documentation.

8. **Recommend actions:** Develop recommendations for actions to be taken based on the findings of the investigation, including any changes to policies or procedures.

9. **Communicate findings and recommendations:** Communicate the findings and recommendations of the investigation to relevant parties, such as management or legal authorities.

10. **Follow-up:** Monitor the implementation of any recommended actions and conduct follow-up investigations if necessary to ensure that the issue has been resolved.

Steps for Evaluating Information

1. **Gather all available information:** Collect all available information about the person's background, including any criminal history, employment history, and references.

2. **Assess the credibility of the sources:** Evaluate the credibility of the sources of information, such as references or official records.

3. **Analyze the information:** Analyze the information gathered from the sources, considering any biases or limitations that may affect the accuracy and relevance of the information.

4. **Identify any red flags or warning signs:** Identify any red flags or warning signs that may indicate potential safety concerns, such as a history of violent behavior or substance abuse.

5. **Consider any mitigating factors:** Consider any mitigating factors that may reduce the likelihood of safety concerns, such as evidence of rehabilitation or a supportive network of family and friends.

6. **Consult with experts or professionals:** Consult with experts or professionals, such as legal or mental health professionals, to help evaluate the information and arrive at a conclusion.

7. **Draw a conclusion:** Based on the analysis and synthesis of the information, draw a conclusion as to whether the person is safe or not.

8. **Communicate the conclusion:** Communicate the conclusion clearly and effectively, providing any necessary context or explanation.

9. **Take appropriate action:** If safety concerns are identified, take appropriate action, such as reporting the concerns to the authorities or seeking legal or professional help.

10. **Reflect on the process:** Reflect on the evaluation process and consider any limitations, biases, or gaps in the information or analysis that may have affected the conclusion.

Properly Identifying Red Flags

1. **Identify your personal boundaries:** Determine your own personal boundaries and expectations for a healthy relationship, such as trust, communication, respect, and mutual support.

2. **Pay attention to your instincts:** Trust your instincts and pay attention to any feelings of discomfort or unease that may arise when interacting with the other person.

3. **Observe their behavior:** Observe the other person's behavior and actions, looking for any behaviors that may indicate potential red flags, such as controlling or manipulative behavior.

4. **Identify any inconsistencies:** Identify any inconsistencies or discrepancies in their behavior or statements, as this may indicate a lack of honesty or trustworthiness.

5. **Evaluate their communication:** Evaluate their communication skills, looking for any signs of poor communication or lack of respect for your feelings and opinions.

6. **Consider their past behavior:** Consider their past behavior and relationships, looking for any patterns or history of problematic behavior.

7. **Observe their response to conflict:** Observe how they handle conflict and disagreements, looking for any signs of aggression, manipulation, or avoidance.

8. **Evaluate their level of commitment:** Evaluate their level of commitment and investment in the relationship, looking for any signs of inconsistency or lack of effort.

9. **Pay attention to how they treat others:** Pay attention to how they treat others, such as friends, family, and service workers, as this can be a reflection of their values and character.

10. **Seek advice from trusted friends or professionals:** Seek advice from trusted friends or professionals, such as a therapist or counselor, who can offer an objective perspective on the relationship.

11. **Reflect on your own feelings and needs:** Reflect on your own feelings and needs, and consider whether the relationship is meeting your own personal boundaries and expectations.

12. **Take action if necessary:** If red flags are identified, take appropriate action to address the concerns, such as having an open and honest conversation with the other person or ending the relationship.

80 Potential Red Flags to Consider When Meeting A Person, Dating, Considering A Relationship, Marriage, or Having A Child

☐ Lack of respect or consideration for others' feelings, opinions, or boundaries.

☐ Unwillingness to compromise or work through problems in a relationship.

☐ Controlling behavior, such as monitoring phone calls, texts, or social media accounts.

☐ Jealousy or possessiveness that goes beyond normal boundaries.

☐ Lying or being dishonest about important issues.

☐ Manipulation or emotional blackmail to get what they want.

☐ Anger issues that lead to outbursts or violent behavior.

☐ Lack of empathy for others' feelings or experiences.

☐ Substance abuse or addiction that affects their behavior or relationships.

☐ Financial irresponsibility or dishonesty.

☐ Infidelity or a history of cheating in past relationships.

☐ Narcissistic or self-centered behavior that puts their needs above others'.

☐   Low self-esteem or constant need for validation from others.

☐   Inability to take responsibility for their actions or behavior.

☐   Poor communication skills, such as being unable to express feelings or listen to others.

☐   Inflexibility or unwillingness to try new things or compromise.

☐   Overly critical or judgmental of others.

☐   Isolation or limiting contact with friends or family.

☐   Lack of ambition or motivation to improve their life or relationships.

☐   Unresolved emotional or mental health issues that affect their behavior or relationships.

☐   Consistent disregard for laws or rules.

☐   Racism, sexism, or other forms of discrimination.

☐   Repeatedly breaking promises or commitments.

☐   Emotional or physical abuse.

☐   Refusal to seek help for personal issues or problems in the relationship.

☐   Inability to handle stress or conflict in a healthy way.

- ☐ Refusal to apologize or make amends for past mistakes.

- ☐ Inability to maintain healthy relationships with friends or family.

- ☐ Extreme need for control or power in the relationship.

- ☐ Inability to express or handle emotions in a healthy way.

- ☐ Irresponsibility or lack of accountability in daily life.

- ☐ Unwillingness to communicate about sex or sexual boundaries.

- ☐ Secretiveness or lack of transparency about important issues.

- ☐ Isolation from society or social circles.

- ☐ Belittling or demeaning language towards others.

- ☐ Constant need for attention or validation from others.

- ☐ Inconsistent or unstable behavior.

- ☐ Extreme mood swings or emotional volatility.

- ☐ Inability to hold down a job or maintain financial stability.

- ☐ Excessive need for privacy or lack of transparency.

- ☐ Refusal to compromise or work through conflicts.

☐ Inability to commit to a long-term relationship.

☐ Extreme pickiness or superficiality in partner selection.

☐ Frequent breakups or relationship instability.

☐ Isolation from or conflict with family members.

☐ Extreme or rigid beliefs that may cause problems in the relationship.

☐ Avoidance of important topics or issues.

☐ Lack of reciprocity or one-sided behavior in the relationship.

☐ Inability to take criticism or feedback

☐ Substance abuse or addiction issues.

☐ Consistently breaking promises or commitments.

☐ Refusal to compromise or work together to solve problems.

☐ Dishonesty or lying about important matters.

☐ History of cheating or infidelity in past relationships.

☐ Secretive or evasive behavior, refusing to answer direct questions.

☐ Unwillingness to discuss or plan for the future.

☐ Poor communication skills, unable to express their thoughts or feelings effectively.

☐ Financial irresponsibility, such as racking up debt or spending frivolously.

☐ Lack of respect for boundaries or personal space.

☐ Jealous or possessive behavior, accusing their partner of flirting or cheating without cause.

☐ Inability to apologize or take responsibility for their mistakes.

☐ Consistently putting their own needs and desires above those of their partner.

☐ Temper outbursts or anger management issues.

☐ Narcissistic tendencies, such as an inflated sense of self-importance or entitlement.

☐ Extreme or irrational jealousy or insecurity.

☐ Lack of ambition or drive to succeed in life.

☐ Incompatibility in core values or beliefs.

☐ Avoidant or dismissive attachment style, showing a lack of emotional intimacy or willingness to connect with their partner.

☐ Entitlement or a belief that they are owed something from others.

☐ Refusal to seek help or counseling for personal issues or problems in the relationship.

☐ Defensiveness or inability to receive constructive criticism.

☐ Refusal to compromise on major life decisions or important matters.

☐ Gaslighting or manipulating their partner into doubting their own perception of reality.

☐ Inability to take criticism or respond to feedback without becoming defensive.

☐ Scapegoating or blaming others for their own problems or mistakes.

☐ Unwillingness to take responsibility for their actions or to apologize when in the wrong.

☐ Blaming others for their problems or failures, rather than taking accountability.

☐ Being overly controlling or possessive.

☐ Disrespectful or dismissive behavior towards people in service positions (e.g. waitstaff, janitors, etc.).

☐ Making derogatory or offensive comments about marginalized groups (e.g. racist, sexist, homophobic, transphobic remarks).

www.ingramcontent.com/pod-product-compliance
Lightning Source LLC
Chambersburg PA
CBHW032050020426
42335CB00011B/276